First Japanese Reader for Students

Miku Ono

First Japanese Reader for Students

Bilingual for Speakers of English

Levels A1 and A2

First Japanese Reader for Students
by Miku Ono
Audio tracks www.lppbooks.com/Japanese/FJRS/En/

Homepage www.audiolego.com

Graphics: Audiolego Design
Images: Canstockphoto

Copyright © 2017 2021 Language Practice Publishing
Copyright © 2017 2021 Audiolego
This book is in copyright. Subject to statutory exception and to the provisions of relevant collective licensing agreements, no reproduction of any part may take place without the written permission of Language Practice Publishing.

目次
Table of contents

How to control the playing speed 6

Pronunciation 7

Chapter 1 The kitchen 10

Chapter 2 Where is the dining room? 21

Chapter 3 The hall 30

Chapter 4 The bathroom 38

Chapter 5 Can you speak German or Spanish? 45

Chapter 6 Can you help me? 53

Chapter 7 What's your name? 64

Chapter 8 The way to university 76

Chapter 9 I like going to the movies 85

Chapter 10 Jack wants to be a lawyer 97

Chapter 11 Jack is sick 113

Chapter 12 Jack wants to find a new apartment 125

Chapter 13 In the store 141

Chapter 14 I have four classes today 153

Chapter 15 Jack wants to work part-time 169

日英辞書 Japanese-English dictionary 179

英日辞書 English-Japanese dictionary 192

Recommended books 206

How to control the playing speed

The book is equipped with the audio tracks. The address of the home page of the book on the Internet, where audio files are available for listening and downloading, is listed at the beginning of the book on the bibliographic description page before the copyright notice. With the help of QR codes, you can call up an audio file in no time, without typing a web address manually. Simply hold your smartphone with camera app on over the QR code. Your smartphone will scan the code and will offer you to follow the scanned audio file link.

We recommend using free **VLC media player** to control the playing speed. You can control the playing speed by decreasing or increasing the speed value on the button of the VLC media player's interface.

Pronunciation

Hiragana	Katakana	Romaji	Hiragana	Katakana	Romaji
あ	ア	a	しゃ	シャ	sha / sya
い	イ	i	しゅ	シュ	shu / syu
う	ウ	u	しょ	ショ	sho / syo
え	エ	e	た	タ	ta
お	オ	o	ち	チ	chi / ti
や	ヤ	ya	つ	ツ	tsu / tu
ゆ	ユ	yu	て	テ	te
よ	ヨ	yo	と	ト	to
か	カ	ka	ちゃ	チャ	cha / tya
き	キ	ki	ちゅ	チュ	chu / tyu
く	ク	ku	ちょ	チョ	cho / tyo
け	ケ	ke	な	ナ	na
こ	コ	ko	に	ニ	ni
きゃ	キャ	kya	ぬ	ヌ	nu
きゅ	キュ	kyu	ね	ネ	ne
きょ	キョ	kyo	の	ノ	no
さ	サ	sa	にゃ	ニャ	nya
し	シ	shi / si	にゅ	ニュ	nyu
す	ス	su	にょ	ニョ	nyo
せ	セ	se	は	ハ	ha
そ	ソ	so	ひ	ヒ	hi

Hiragana	Katakana	Romaji	Hiragana	Katakana	Romaji
ふ	フ	fu / hu	ろ	ロ	ro
へ	ヘ	he	りゃ	リャ	rya
ほ	ホ	ho	りゅ	リュ	ryu
ひゃ	ヒャ	hya	りょ	リョ	ryo
ひゅ	ヒュ	hyu	わ	ワ	wa
ひょ	ヒョ	hyo	ゐ	ヰ	i / wi / i
ま	マ	ma	ゑ	ヱ	e / we / e
み	ミ	mi	を	ヲ	o / wo / o
む	ム	mu	ん	ン	n-n'(-m) / n-n'
め	メ	me	が	ガ	ga
も	モ	mo	ぎ	ギ	gi
みゃ	ミャ	mya	ぐ	グ	gu
みゅ	ミュ	myu	げ	ゲ	ge
みょ	ミョ	myo	ご	ゴ	go
や	ヤ	ya	ぎゃ	ギャ	gya
ゆ	ユ	yu	ぎゅ	ギュ	gyu
よ	ヨ	yo	ぎょ	ギョ	gyo
ら	ラ	ra	ざ	ザ	za
り	リ	ri	じ	ジ	ji / zi
る	ル	ru	ず	ズ	zu
れ	レ	re	ぜ	ゼ	ze

Hiragana	Katakana	Romaji	Hiragana	Katakana	Romaji
ぞ	ゾ	zo	ぶ	ブ	bu
じゃ	ジャ	ja / zya	べ	ベ	be
じゅ	ジュ	ju / zyu	ぼ	ボ	bo
じょ	ジョ	jo / zyo	びゃ	ビャ	bya
だ	ダ	da	びゅ	ビュ	byu
ぢ	ヂ	ji / di / zi	びょ	ビョ	byo
づ	ヅ	zu / du / zu	ぱ	パ	pa
で	デ	de	ぴ	ピ	pi
ど	ド	do	ぷ	プ	pu
ぢゃ	ヂャ	ja / dya / zya	ぺ	ペ	pe
ぢゅ	ヂュ	ju / dyu / zyu	ぽ	ポ	po
ぢょ	ヂョ	jo / dyo / zyo	ぴゃ	ピャ	pya
ば	バ	ba	ぴゅ	ピュ	pyu
び	ビ	bi	ぴょ	ピョ	pyo

1

Audio

氷を砕く
Break the ice

"ママ、今日ぼくは勇敢だったんだ！"と幼い男の子はお母さんに言いました。"大きな、生きてる虫を見てたんだけど逃げ出さなかったんだ！"

mama, kyō boku wa yūkan datta n da! to osanai otokonoko wa okāsan ni iimashita. ōkina, ikiteru mushi o miteta n da kedo nigedasanakatta n da!

"Mom, I was brave today!" a little boy says to his mom. "I was looking at a big, live bug and I did not run away!"

キッチン
The kitchen

A

単語
Words

1. 〜から、〜の外へ [〜kara, 〜no sotohe] - from, out of
2. 〜と一緒に [〜to isshoni] - with
3. 〜にある、〜がある [〜ni aru, 〜ga aru] - there is, there are
4. 〜に位置する, 〜にある [〜ni ichisuru, 〜niaru] - be (located)
5. 〜に入る [〜ni hairu] - go into
6. 〜のため、〜にとって [〜notame, 〜nitotte] - for
7. 〜の近く、〜のそば [〜no chikaku, no soba] - near
8. 〜の後ろ、〜のため [〜no ushiro, 〜no tame] - behind, for
9. 〜の向かいに [〜no mukaini] - across from
10. 〜の上 [〜no ue] - on
11. 〜の中 [〜no naka] - in
12. 〜も [〜mo] - also, too
13. いいえ;〜は(が)ない [iie, 〜ha(ga) nai] - no; there isn't, there aren't
14. かける、かかる、つるさがる [kakeru, kakaru, tsurusagaru] - hang
15. かわいい、美しい [kawaii, utsukushii] - pretty, beautiful
16. きれい、きれいにする [kirei, kireinisuru] - clean
17. これ [kore] - this
18. そして [soshite] - and
19. どこ [doko] - where
20. にわとり、チキン [niwatori, chikin] - chicken

21. ぬくもりのある、心地の良い [nukumorinoaru, kokochinoyoi] - cozy, comfortable
22. ねこ [neko] - cat
23. はい [hai] - yes
24. または [mataha] - or
25. カップボード、たんす、本棚 [kappubo-do, tansu] - cupboard, wardrobe, bookcase
26. ガス [gasu] - gas
27. ガラス [garasu] - glass
28. キッチン [kicchin] - kitchen
29. グレー [gure-] - gray
30. コーヒーメーカー [ko-hi-me-ka-] - coffeemaker
31. コップ [koppu] - cup
32. ゴム [gomu] - rubber
33. シャンデリア [shanderia] - chandelier
34. シンク [sinku] - sink
35. スタンド [sutando] - stand
36. ストーブ [suto-bu] - stove
37. スプーン [supu-n] - spoon
38. テーブル [te-buru] - table
39. テーブルクロス [te-burukurosu] - tablecloth
40. ティーポット [ti-potto] - teapot
41. トースター [to-suta-] - toaster
42. ドア [doa] - door
43. ドライヤー [doraiya-] - dryer
44. ナプキン [napukin] - napkin
45. ハンドル [handoru] - handle
46. フォーク [fo-ku] - fork
47. ブレンダー [burenda-] - blender
48. ミキサー [mikisa-] - mixer
49. 椅子 [isu] - chair
50. 飲む [nomu] - drink
51. 右に [migini] - on the right
52. 汚い [kitanai] - dirty
53. 黄色 [kiiro] - yellow
54. 屋根 [yane] - roof
55. 何 [nani] - what
56. 家 [ie] - house
57. 家で [iede] - at home
58. 花 [hana] - flower
59. 海 [umi] - sea
60. 角 [kado] - corner
61. 丸い [marui] - round
62. 気を付ける、注意する [ki wo tsukeru, chuuisuru] - careful
63. 魚 [sakana] - fish
64. 金属 [kinzoku] - metal
65. 犬 [inu] - dog
66. 古い [furui] - old
67. 光 [hikari] - light
68. 広い [hiroi] - spacious
69. 紅茶 [koucha] - tea
70. 左に [hidarini] - on the left
71. 皿、プレート [sara, pure-to] - plate
72. 私たち [watashitachi] - we
73. 写真、絵 [shashin, e] - picture
74. 小さい [chiisai] - small
75. 上に [ueni] - on top of, over, above
76. 食器 [shokki] - dishes
77. 心地の良い [kokochinoyoi] - comfortable
78. 新しい [atarashii] - new
79. 水 [mizu] - water
80. 赤 [aka] - red

81. 洗濯機、〜洗機、洗っている [sentakuki, 〜senki, aratteiru] - washer, washing
82. 船 [fune] - ship
83. 窓 [mado] - window
84. 走る [hashiru] - run
85. 大きい [ookii] - big
86. 町 [machi] - city
87. 庭 [niwa] - garden
88. 天井 [tenjou] - ceiling
89. 盗む [nusumu] - steal
90. 踏みつける [fumitsukeru] - trample
91. 道、道路 [michi, douro] - street
92. 白 [shiro] - white
93. 彼/彼女/それ [kare/kanojo/sore] - he/she/it
94. 壁 [kabe] - wall
95. 木製の [mokuseino] - wooden
96. 欲しい [hoshii] - want
97. 緑 [midori] - green
98. 冷蔵庫 [reizouko] - refrigerator
99. 廊下 [rouka] - hall

B

これは町です。それは大きくて美しいです。それは海の近くに位置しています。
kore wa machi desu. sore wa ōkikute utsukushii desu. sore wa umi no chikaku ni ichishiteimasu.

This is a city. It is big and beautiful. It is located near the sea.

これは道です。それは町の中にあります。道は大きくてきれいです。
kore wa michi desu. sore wa machi no nakani arimasu. michi wa ōkikute kirei desu.

This is a street. It is in the city. The street is large and clean.

これは家です。家は道に建っています。それはきちんとしていて美しいです。壁は白です。屋根は赤です。ドアは新しいです。それは木製です。
kore wa ie desu. ie wa michi ni tatteimasu. sore wa kichinto shiteite utsukushii desu. kabe wa shiro desu.

This is a house. The house is in the street. It is neat and beautiful. The walls are white. The roof is red. The door is new. It is wooden.

yane wa aka desu. doa wa atarashii desu. sore wa mokusei desu.

これは庭です。庭は家の近くに位置します。それは大きくて緑です。犬が庭でにわとりを追いかけています。それは花を踏みつけています。

kore wa niwa desu. niwa wa ie no chikaku ni ichishimasu. sore wa ōkikute midori desu. inu ga niwa de niwatori o oikaketeimasu. sore wa hana o fumitsuketeimasu.

私たちは家の中に入ります。これは廊下です。廊下は広くそして心地が良いです。

watashitachi wa ie no nakani hairimasu. kore wa rōka desu. rōka wa hiroku soshite kokochi ga yoi desu.

キッチンは右にあります。キッチンは大きくて明るいです。壁は黄色です。天井は白です。天井にシャンデリアがあります。それは大きくて美しいです。

kitchin wa migi ni arimasu. kitchin wa ōkikute akarui desu. kabe wa kiiro desu. tenjō wa shiro desu. tenjō ni shanderia ga arimasu. sore wa ōkikute utsukushii desu.

これはテーブルです。それは大きくて丸いです。テーブルにはテーブルクロスがあります。

kore wa te-buru desu. sore wa ōkikute marui desu. te-buru ni wa te-burukurosu ga arimasu.

これはミキサーです。それはテーブルの上にありま

This is a garden. The garden is located near the house. It's big and green. A dog is running after a chicken in the garden. It tramples on flowers.

We go into the house. This is a hall. The hall is spacious and comfortable.

The kitchen is on the right. The kitchen is large and bright. The walls are yellow. The ceiling is white. There is a chandelier on the ceiling. It is big and beautiful.

This is a table. It's big and round. There is a tablecloth on the table.

This is a mixer. It is on the table. It's comfortable and

す。それは心地よくて小さいです。
kore wa mikisa- desu. sore wa te-buru no ueni arimasu. sore wa kokochiyokute chiisai desu.

これはグラスです。それもテーブルの上にあります。それはガラスでできています。そのグラスはきれいです。
kore wa gurasu desu. sore mo te-buru no ueni arimasu. sore wa garasu de dekiteimasu. sono gurasu wa kirei desu.

テーブルの近くに椅子があります。それは木製です。その椅子は座り心地がよいです。
te-buru no chikaku ni isu ga arimasu. sore wa mokusei desu. sono isu wa suwarigokochi ga yoi desu.

これは冷蔵庫です。それはグレーです。その冷蔵庫は新しいです。それは角に位置します。その冷蔵庫の近くにはねこがいます。彼は冷蔵庫から魚を盗みたいと考えています。
kore wa reizōko desu. sore wa gure- desu. sono reizōko wa atarashii desu. sore wa kaku ni ichishimasu. sono reizōko no chikaku ni wa neko ga imasu. kare wa reizōko kara sakana o nusumitai to kangaeteimasu.

これはトースターです。それは冷蔵庫の上にあります。そのトースターは小さくて便利です。
kore wa to-suta- desu. sore wa reizōko no ueni arimasu. sono to-suta- wa chiisakute benri desu.

small.

This is a glass. It is also on the table. It is made of glass. The glass is clean.

Near the table there is a chair. It is wooden. The chair is comfortable.

This is a refrigerator. It is gray. The refrigerator is new. It is located in the corner. There is a cat near the refrigerator. He wants to steal fish from the refrigerator.

This is a toaster. It is standing on the refrigerator. The toaster is small and convenient.

これはコーヒーメーカーです。それはシンクの近くにあります。そのコーヒーメーカーは汚いです。
これはブレンダーです。それも冷蔵庫の上にあります。それは白いです。そのブレンダーは古いです。

kore wa ko-hi- me-ka- desu. sore wa shinku no chikaku ni arimasu. sono ko-hi- me-ka- wa kitanai desu. kore wa burenda- desu. sore mo reizōko no ueni arimasu. sore wa shiroi desu. sono burenda- wa furui desu.

冷蔵庫の向かいに窓があります。それは大きくてきれいです。

reizōko no mukai ni mado ga arimasu. sore wa ōkikute kirei desu.

これはストーブです。窓の近くに位置します。それは新しくて便利です。

kore wa suto-bu desu. mado no chikaku ni ichishimasu. sore wa atarashikute benri desu.

これはケトルです。それはガスストーブの上にあります。それは金属でゴムのハンドルが付いています。

kore wa ketoru desu. sore wa gasu suto-bu no ueni arimasu. sore wa kinzoku de gomu no handoru ga tsuiteimasu.

冷蔵庫の近くには食洗器があります。
左には、食器のためのドライヤーがあります。

reizōko no chikaku ni wa shoku araiki ga arimasu. hidari

This is a coffee maker. It is standing near the sink. The coffee maker is dirty.

This is a blender. It is also on the refrigerator. It is white. The blender is old.

There is a window across from the refrigerator. It is large and clean.

This is a stove. It is located near the window. It is new and convenient.

This is a kettle. It is on a gas stove. It is metal with a rubber handle.

Near the refrigerator there is a dishwasher. To the left, there is a dryer for dishes.

ni wa, shokki no tame no doraiya- ga arimasu.

これはカップボードです。シンクの上にあります。
それは木製です。

kore wa kappu bo-do desu. shinku no ueni arimasu. sore wa mokusei desu.

これはナプキンです。それはキッチンのカップボードの中にあります。それは小さくてきれいです。

kore wa napukin desu. sore wa kitchin no kappu bo-do no nakani arimasu. sore wa chiisakute kirei desu.

これは写真です。それは壁にかけてあります。
絵の中には海と船があります。

kore wa shashin desu. sore wa kabe nikakete arimasu. e no nakani wa umi to fune ga arimasu.

これはキッチンテーブルです。それは角に位置します。それは大きくて木製です。

kore wa kitchin te-buru desu. sore wa kaku ni ichishimasu. sore wa ōkikute mokusei desu.

これはフォークです。それはテーブルのうえにあります。フォークは金属です。それはきれいです。

kore wa fuxo-ku desu. sore wa te-buru no ueni arimasu. fuxo-ku wa kinzoku desu. sore wa kirei desu.

これは皿です。それはキッチンテーブルの上にあります。その皿は黄色です。それは小さくて美しいです。

kore wa sara desu. sore wa kitchin te-buru no ueni

	This is a cupboard. It hangs over the sink. It is wooden.
	This is a napkin. It is in the kitchen cupboard. It's small and clean.
	This is a picture. It is on the wall. There is the sea and a ship in the painting.
	This is the kitchen table. It is located in the corner. It is large and wooden.
	This is a fork. It is on the table. The fork is metal. It is clean.
	This is a dish. It is on the kitchen table. The plate is yellow. It's small and beautiful.

arimasu. sono sara wa kiiro desu. sore wa chiisakute utsukushii desu.

これはコップです。それもキッチンテーブルの上にあります。そのコップは赤です。ねこはそのコップから水を飲みます。

kore wa koppu desu. sore mo kitchin te-buru no ueni arimasu. sono koppu wa aka desu. neko wa sono koppu kara mizu o nomimasu.

This is a cup. It is also on the kitchen table. The cup is red. A cat drinks water from the cup.

これはティースプーンです。それはコップの中に位置します。そのスプーンは金属です。それは小さいです。

kore wa thi-supu-n desu. sore wa koppu no nakani ichishimasu. sono supu-n wa kinzoku desu. sore wa chiisai desu.

This is a teaspoon. It is located in a cup. The spoon is metal. It's small.

C

質問と答え

- 町はどこですか？
- 海の近くに位置します。
- 道は大きいですかそれとも小さいですか？ - 道は大きいです。
- 家はどこですか？
- 家は道にあります。

Questions and answers

- Where is the city?
- It is located near the sea.
- Is the street big or small?
- The street is big.
- Where is the house?
- The house is in the street.
- Where is the garden?
- The garden is located near the house.

にわ
- 庭はどこにありますか？
- 庭は家の近くに位置します。
- 庭は大きいですかそれとも小さいですか？ - 庭は大きいです。
- 廊下は広いですか？
- はい、廊下は広いです。
- きっちんはどこですか？
- きっちんは右にあります。
- みきさーはどこですか？
- みきさーはてーぶるの上にあります。
- てーぶるくろすはてーぶるの上にありますか？ - はい、てーぶるくろすはてーぶるの上にあります。
- てーぶるの上には何がありますか？
- てーぶるの上にはぐらすがあります。
- それは汚いですか？
- いいえ、ぐらすはきれいです。
- 冷蔵庫はどこですか？
- 冷蔵庫は角にあります。
- ねこはどこですか？
- ねこは冷蔵庫の近くにいます。
- こーひーめーかーはどこですか？

- The garden is large or small?
- The garden is large.
- Is the hall spacious?
- Yes, the hall is spacious.
- Where's the kitchen?
- Kitchen is on the right.
- Where is the mixer?
- The mixer on the table.
- Is there a tablecloth on the table?
- Yes, there is a tablecloth on the table.
- What is there on the table?
- There is a glass on the table.
- It is dirty?
- No, the glass is clean.
- Where's the fridge?
- The refrigerator is in the corner.
- Where is the cat?
- The cat is near the refrigerator.
- Where is coffeemaker?
- The coffeemaker is near the sink.
- Is the coffeemaker clean?

−こーひーめーかーはしんくの近くにあります。 −こーひーめーかーはきれいですか？
−いいえ、それは汚いです。
−きっちんの中に窓はありますか？
−はい、窓は冷蔵庫の向かい側にあります。
−窓は大きいですか？
−はい、それは大きいです。
−ふぉーくはどこですか？
−ふぉーくはきっちんてーぶるの上にあります。
−皿もきっちんてーぶるの上にありますか？
−はい、皿はきっちんてーぶるの上にあります。
−なぷきんはきっちんの中にありますか？
−はい、なぷきんはきっちんのかっぷぼーどの中にあります。
−きれいなこっぷはきっちんにありますか？
−はい、きれいなこっぷはてーぶるの上にあります。
−こっぷは赤いですか？
−はい、それは赤いです。

- No, it's dirty.
- Is there a window in the kitchen?
- Yes, the window is across from the refrigerator.
- Is the window large?
- Yes, it's large.
- Where is the fork?
- The fork is on the kitchen table.
- Is the plate also on the kitchen table?
- Yes, a plate is on the kitchen table.
- Are there napkins in the kitchen?
- Yes, there are napkins in the kitchen cupboard.
- Is there a clean cup in the kitchen?
- Yes, the clean cup is on the table.
- Is the cup red?
- Yes, it is red.

2

Audio

氷(こおり)を砕(くだ)く
Break the ice

幼(おさな)い二人(ににん)の少年(しょうねん)が話(はな)しています。

"弟(おとうと)の名前(なまえ)どうやって決(き)めた?"と一人(いちにん)の男(おとこ)の子(こ)が聞(き)きます。

"僕(ぼく)はばっとまんって名前(なまえ)が良(よ)かったんだけど、ぱぱとままがとむって名前(なまえ)にしたんだ。"と深(ふか)くため息(いき)をつきながら答(こた)えました。

Two little boys are talking.

"How did you name your younger brother?" one of them asks the other.

"I wanted to name him Batman," the boy answered and sighed deeply, "but my parents named him Tom."

osanai ni nin no shōnen ga hanashiteimasu. otōto no namae dō yatte kimeta? to ichi nin no otokonoko ga kikimasu. boku wa Battoman tte namae ga yokatta n da kedo, papa to mama ga Tomu tte namae ni shita n da. to fukaku tameiki o tsuki nagara kotaemashita.

ダイニングルームはどこですか？
Where is the dining room?

A

単語
Words

1. 3、三 [san, san] - three
2. 4、四 [yon, yon] - four
3. 6、六 [roku, roku] - six
4. 〜でない [〜denai] - not
5. かびん [kabin] - vase
6. ここ [koko] - here
7. これ [kore] - this
8. これら(複数) [korera (fukusuu)] - these (plural)
9. どれ、何 [dore, nani] - which, what
10. どれくらい、いくら [dorekurai, ikura] - how much
11. カーペット [ka-petto] - carpet
12. ダイニングルーム [daininguru-mu] - dining room
13. ナイフ [naifu] - knife
14. プラスチック [purasuchikku] - plastic
15. 鏡 [kagami] - mirror
16. 空 [kara] - empty
17. 座る [suwaru] - sit
18. 床 [yuka] - floor
19. 色 [iro] - color
20. 新しい [atarashii] - new
21. 青 [ao] - blue
22. 赤 [aka] - red
23. 棚、シェルフ [tana, sherufu] - shelf
24. 茶色 [chairo] - brown
25. 入る [hairu] - enter
26. 白 [shiro] - white
27. 彼ら(複数) [karera (fukusuu)] - they
28. 部屋 [heya] - room
29. 腕時計 [udedokei] - watch

B

-これがきっちんですか？
-kore ga kicchin desuka?
-はい、これはキッチンです。
-hai, kore ha kicchin desu.
-ダイニングルームはどこですか？
-daininguru-mu ha doko desuka?
-だいにんぐるーむは 左 にあります。
-daininguru-mu ha hidari ni arimasu.
-私 たちはだいにんぐるーむに 入 ります。
-watashitachi ha daininguru-mu ni hairi masu.
-これは 何 ですか？
-kore ha nandesuka?
-これはテーブルです。
-kore ha te-buru desu.
-テーブルはプラスチックですか？
-te-buru ha purasuchikku desuka?
-いいえ、それは木でできています。
-iie, sore ha ki de dekite imasu.
- 机 の 上 には 何 がありますか？
-tsukue no ue niha nani ga arimasuka?
-これらは 皿 とすぷーんです。
-korera ha sara to supu-n ga desu.
-それらはきれいですか？
-sorera ha kirei desuka?
-はい、それらはきれいです。
-hai, sorera ha kirei desu.
-テーブルのそばにはなにがありますか？
-te-buru no soba niha nani ga arimasuka?

- Is this the kitchen?
- Yes, this is the kitchen.
- Where is the dining room?
- The dining room is to the left.
We enter the dining room.
- What is this?
- This is a table.
- Is the table plastic?
- No, it is made of wood.
- What is there on the table?
- These are plates and spoons.
- Are they clean?
- Yes, they are clean.

- これは椅子です。
- kore ha isu desu.
- それは新しいですか？
- sore ha atarashii desuka?
- はい、それは新しくて座り心地が良いです。
- hai, sore ha atarashiku te suwarigokochi ga ii desu.
- 椅子は何色ですか？
- isu ha naniiro desuka?
- 椅子の色は茶色です。
- isu no iro ha chairo desu.
- この部屋の中にはいくつ椅子がありますか？
- kono heya no naka niha ikutsu isu ga arimasuka?
- この部屋の中には椅子が4つがあります。
- kono heya no naka niha isu ga yottsu arimasu.
- コップはどこですか？
- koppu ha doko desuka?
- こっぷはてーぶるの上にあります。
- koppu ha te-buru no ue ni arimasu.
- てぃーけとるはどこにありますか？
- ti-ketoru ha doko ni arimasuka?
- けとるはすとーぶの上にあります。
- ketoru ha suto-bu no ue ni arimasu.
- それは空ですか？
- soreha kara desuka?
- いいえ、それは空ではありません。ねこがてぃーぽっとの上にいます。

- What is there at the table?
- This is a chair.
- Is it new?
- Yes, it is new and comfortable.
- What color is this chair?
- This chair is brown.
- How many chairs are in this room?
- There are four chairs in this room.
- Where are the cups?
- The cups are on the table.
- Where is the tea kettle?
- The kettle is on the stove.
- Is it empty?
- No, it is not empty. The cat is

-iie, soreha kara deha arimasen. neko ga ti-potto no ue ni imasu.
- 壁には何がかけてありますか？
-kabe niha nani ga kakete arimasuka?
-それは絵です。
-sore ha e desu.
-絵は新しいですかそれとも古いですか？
-e ha atarashi desuka soretomo furui desuka?
-それは美しくて古いです。
-sore ha utsukushikute furui desu.
-ナプキンはどこですか？
-napukin ha doko desuka?
-なぷきんは戸棚にあります。
-napukin ha todana ni arimasu.
-戸棚はどこにありますか？
-todana ha doko ni arimasuka?
-それは絵の近くに立っています。
-sore ha e no chikaku ni tatte imasu.
-戸棚は何色ですか？
-todana ha naniiro desuka?
-それは白です。
-sore ha shiro desu.
-戸棚にはいくつ棚がありますか？
-todana niha ikutsu tana ga arimasuka?
-戸棚には3つ棚があります。
-todana niha mittsu tana ga arimasu.
-ふぉーくはどこにありますか？
-fo-ku ha doko ni arimasuka?

sitting in the teapot.
- What is hanging on the wall?
- It is a picture.
- Is the picture new or old?
- It is beautiful and old.
- Where are the napkins?
- The napkins are in a cabinet.
- Where is the cabinet?
- It is standing near the picture.
- What color is the cabinet?
- It is white.
- How many shelves are there in the cabinet?
- The cabinet has three shelves.

-ふぉーくも戸棚の中にあります。
-fo-ku mo todana no naka ni arimasu.
-これは何ですか？
-kore ha nan desuka?
-これは鏡です。犬が鏡をのぞいています。
-kore ha kagami desu. inu ga kagami wo nozoite imasu.
-床の上には何がありますか？
-yuka no ue ni ha nani ga arimasuka?
-これはカーペットです。
-kore ha ka-petto desu.
-このかーぺっとは何色ですか？
-kono ka-petto ha naniiro desuka?
-このかーぺっとは青です。
-kono ka-petto ha ao desu.
-天井は何色ですか？
-tenjou ha naniiro desuka?
-天井はぐれーです。
-tenjou ha gure- desu.
-天井には何がつるさがっていますか？
-tenjou niha nani ga tsurusagatte imasuka?
-これはしゃんでりあです。
-kore ha shanderia desu.
-このしゃんでりあは何色ですか？
-kono shanderia ha naniiro desuka?
-このしゃんでりあは青と白です。
-kono shanderia ha ao to shiro desu.

- Where are the forks?
- The forks are also in the cabinet.
- What is this?
- This is a mirror. The dog is looking in the mirror.
- What's on the floor?
- This is a carpet.
- What color is this carpet?
- This carpet is blue.
- What color is the ceiling?
- The ceiling is gray.
- What is hanging on the ceiling?
- This is a chandelier.
- What color is this chandelier?

- 冷蔵庫はどこですか？
-reizouko ha doko desuka?
-きっちんの中にあります。
-kicchin no naka ni arimasu.
-冷蔵庫は大きいですか？
-reizouko ha ookii desuka?
-はい、それは大きいです。
-hai, sore ha ookii desu.
-冷蔵庫は何色ですか？
-reizouko ha naniiro desuka?
-冷蔵庫はぐれーです。ねこが冷蔵庫から魚を取って食べています。
-reizouko ha gure- desu. neko ga reizouko kara sakana wo totte tabete imasu.
-ぶれんだーはどこですか？
-burenda- ha doko desuka?
-それは冷蔵庫の上にあります。
-sore ha reizouko no ue ni arimasu.
-そのぶれんだーは新しいですか？
-sono burenda- ha atarashii desuka?
-はい、それは新しいです。
-hai, sore ha atarashii desu.
-コーヒーメーカーはどこですか？
-ko-hi-me-ka- ha doko desuka?
-それはしんくの近くにあります。
-sore ha shinku no chikaku ni arimasu.
-コーヒーメーカーはきれいですか？

- This chandelier is blue and white.
- Where is the refrigerator?
- It is located in the kitchen.
- Is the refrigerator big?
- Yes, it's big.
- What color is the refrigerator?
- The refrigerator is gray. The cat is eating fish from the refrigerator.
- Where's the blender?
- It is on the refrigerator.
- Is the blender new?
- Yes, it is new.
- Where is the coffee maker?
- It is near the sink.

-ko-hi-me-ka- ha kirei desuka?
-いいえ、それは汚いです。
-iie, sore ha kitanai desu.
-トースターはどこですか？
-to-suta- ha doko desuka?
-それはきっちんの戸棚の中にあります。
-sore ha kicchin no todana no naka ni arimasu.
-てーぶるの上には何がありますか？
-te-buru no ue niha nani ga arimasuka?
-これはかびんです。
-kore ha kabin desu.
-これはガラスですか？
-kore ha garasu desuka?
-はい、これはガラスです。
-hai, kore ha garasu desu.
-かびんの中には何が立っていますか？
kabin no naka niha nani ga tatte imasuka?
-そこには花があります。
-soko niha hana ga arimasu.
-かびんの中には花が何本ありますか？
-kabin no naka ni ha hana ga nanbon arimasuka?
-かびんの中には花が6本あります。
- kabin no naka ni ha hana ga roppon arimasu.
-これらの花は何色ですか？
-korera no hana ha naniiro desuka?
-それらは赤です。
-sorera ha aka desu.
-ここにミキサーはありますか？

- Is the coffee maker clean?
- No, it's dirty.
- Where is the toaster?
- It is in the kitchen cabinet.
- What is there on the table?
- This is a vase.
- Is it glass?
- Yes, it is glass.
- What is standing in the vase?
- These are flowers there.
- How many flowers are there in the vase?
- There are six flowers in the vase.
- What color are these flowers?
- They are red.
- Is there the mixer

-koko ni mikisa- ha arimasuka?
-いいえ、ミキサーはキッチンにあります。
-iie, mikisa- ha kicchin ni arimasu.
-ないふは戸棚の中にありますか？
-naifu ha todana no naka ni arimasuka?
-はい、ないふは戸棚の中にあります。
-hai, naifu ha todana no naka ni arimasu.
-この食器は何色ですか？
-kono shokki ha naniiro desuka?
-これは青です。
-kore ha ao desu.
-この壁は何色ですか？
-kono kabe ha naniiro desuka?
-これは緑です。
-kore ha midori desu.

here?

- No, the mixer is in the kitchen.

- Are there knives in the cabinet?

- Yes, there are knives in the cabinet.

- What color is this dish?

- It is blue.

- What color is this wall?

- It is green.

3

Audio

氷(こおり)を砕(くだ)く
Break the ice

一人(いちにん)のお母(かあ)さんが息子(むすこ)の様子(ようす)を確認(かくにん)しようと息子(むすこ)の寝室(しんしつ)に入(はい)っていきました。彼(かれ)は床(ゆか)に

A mom comes into the bedroom and sees her little son lying on the floor.

寝転がっています。

"ぽーる、寝ているの？"とお母さんはぽーるに聞きます。

"違うよ、遊んでるんだ"とぽーるは答えました。

それを聞いたお母さんは寝室を後にしました。10分後、様子を見に息子の寝室に戻ってきたのです。彼はまだ、同じ場所に寝転がったままです。

"どんなお遊びをしているの？"とお母さんは息子に聞きました。

"壊れたろぼっとの真似げーむをしているんだ"と彼は言いました。

ichi nin no okāsan ga musuko no yōsu o kakuninshiyou to musuko no shinshitsu ni haitteikimashita. kare wa yuka ni nekorogatteimasu. Po-Ru, neteiru no? to okāsan wa po-ru ni kikimasu. chigau yo, asonderu n da to po-ru wa kotaemashita. sore o kiita okāsan wa shinshitsu ogo ni shimashita. 10 fungo, yōsu o mi ni musuko no shinshitsu ni modottekita no desu. kare wa mada, onaji basho ni nekorogatta mama desu. donna o asobi o shiteiru no? to okāsan wa musuko ni kikimashita. kowareta robotto no mane ge-mu o shiteiru n da to kare wa iimashita.

"Paul, are you sleeping?" the mom asks.

"No. I am playing," the son answers.

The mom goes away. She returns to the bedroom ten minutes later. Her son is lying on the floor in the same place.

"What game are you playing?" she asks.

"I am playing a robot. A broken robot."

廊下
The hall

単語
Words

1. 〜かどうか、もし [〜kadouka, moshi] - whether, if
2. 〜で、〜の近くで、〜のそばで [〜de, 〜no chikakude, 〜no sobade] - at, near
3. 〜の下 [〜no shita] - under
4. 〜も [〜mo] - also
5. だんろ [danro] - fireplace
6. まくら [makura] - pillow
7. もっと、よりおおくの、まだ [motto, yoriookuno, mada] - more, still
8. アームチェア [a-muchea] - armchair
9. コーヒーテーブル [ko-hi-te-buru] - coffee table
10. シェイクスピア [sheikusupia] - Shakespeare
11. スイッチ [suicchi] - switch
12. ソファー、カウチ [sofa-, kauchi] - sofa, couch
13. チューリップ [chu-rippu] - tulip
14. テレビセット [terebisetto] - Tv-set
15. バラ [bara] - rose
16. パス [pasu] - pass
17. ベージュ [be-ju] - beige
18. ラジオ [rajio] - radio
19. ランプ [ranpu] - lamp
20. 横になっている [yokoninatteiru] - lie
21. 近く [chikaku] - near

22. 黒 [kuro] - black
23. 紫 [murasaki] - purple
24. 写真 [shashin] - photograph
25. 柔らかい [yawarakai] - soft
26. 小さなテーブル [chiisanate-buru] - little table
27. 真っすぐ [massugu] - straight
28. 沢山、とても [takusan, totemo] - many, a lot
29. 動く、機能する [ugoku, kinousuru] - work, function
30. 本 [hon] - book
31. 面白い、興味深い [omoshiroi, kyoumibukai] - interesting
32. 廊下、通路 [rouka, tsuuro] - hall

B

ろうか
- 廊下はどこですか？

-rouka ha doko desuka?

ろうか　ま　　　ぜんぽう
- 廊下は真っすぐ前方にあります。

-rouka ha massugu zenpou ni arimasu.

わたし　　　ろうか　いどう　　　　へや　おお
　私たちは廊下に移動します。部屋は大きくそして
いごこち　よ　　　　てんじょう　　　　　　かべ
居心地が良いです。天井はぐれーです。壁は
みどり
　緑です。

Watashitachi ha rouka ni idou shimasu. heya ha ookiku soshite kokochi ga ii desu. tenjou ha gure- desu. kabe ha midori desu.

ゆか　うえ　　なに
- 床の上には何がありますか？

-yuka no ue niha nani ga arimasuka?

ゆか　うえ　　　　　　　　　　　　　　　　　やわ
- 床の上にはかーぺっとがあります。それは柔らかい
　　　　　　　　　　　　　むらさき
です。そのかーぺっとは　紫　です。

-yuka no ue niha ka-petto ga arimasu. sore ha yawarakai desu. Sono ka-petto ha murasaki desu.

　　　　　　　うえ　　なに　た
-かーぺっとの上には何が立っていますか？

-ka-petto no ue niha nani ga tatte imasuka?

- Where is the hall?

- The hall is straight ahead.

We pass into the hall. The room is large and cozy. The ceiling is gray. The walls are green.

- What is there on the floor?

- There is a carpet on the floor. It is soft. The carpet is purple.

- What is standing on the carpet?

- There is a coffee table on the carpet. It is glass. On the table

-かーぺっとの上にはこーひーてーぶるがあります。それはがらすです。てーぶるの上には面白い本があります。それはぐれーです。
-ka-petto no ue niha ko-hi-te-buru ga arimasu. sore ha garasu desu. te-buru no ue niha omoshiroi hon ga arimasu. sore ha gure- desu.
-あーむちぇあはどこですか？
-a-muchea ha doko desuka?
-あーむちぇあはこーひーてーぶるの後ろにあります。それは巨大で座り心地が良いです。
-a-muchea ha ko-hi-te-buru no ushiro ni arimasu.sore ha kyodai de suwarigokochi ga ii desu.
-そふぁーはこの部屋の中にありますか？
-sofa ha kono heya no naka ni arimasuka?
-はい、そふぁーは窓の近くにあります。ねこは魚と一緒にかうちに座っています。それらは紫です。まくらは柔らかく、そして心地が良いです。
-hai, sofa ha mado no chikaku ni arimasu. neko ha sakana to issho ni kauchi ni suwatte imasu. sorera ha murasaki desu. makura ha yawarakaku soshite kokochi ga ii desu.
-壁には何がかけてありますか？
-kabe niha nani ga kakete arimasuka?
-壁には絵がかけてあります。
-kabe ni ha e ga kakete arimasu.
-だんろはこの部屋の中のどこにありますか？
-danro ha kono heya no naka no doko ni arimasuka?

there is an interesting book. It is gray.
- Where is the armchair?
- The armchair is behind the coffee table. It is large and comfortable.
- Is there a sofa in this room?
- Yes, the sofa stands near a window. A cat is sitting on the couch with fish. There are couch cushions lying on the couch as well. They are purple. The pillows are soft and comfortable.
- What is hanging on the wall?
- A picture is hanging on the wall.
- Where is the fireplace in this room?
- The fireplace is located under the

- だんろは絵の下にあります。それは大きくて美しいです。
-danro ha e no shita ni arimasu. sore ha ookikute utsukushii desu.

- まんとるぴーすの上には何がありますか？
-mantorupi-su no ue niha nani ga arimasuka?

- まんとるぴーすの上は写真とかびんがあります。
-mantorupi-su no ue ni ha shashin to kabin ga arimasu.

- かびんの中には何がありますか？
-kabin no naka niha nani ga arimasuka?

- かびんの中には美しい黄色いばらがあります。
- kabin no naka ni ha utsukushii kiiroi bara ga arimasu.

- かびんの中には何本のばらがありますか？
- kabin no naka ni ha nanbon no bara ga arimasuka?

- かびんの中には6本のばらがあります。
- kabin no naka ni ha roppon no bara ga arimasu.

- この部屋の中には花はもっとありますか？
- kono heya no naka ni ha hana ha motto arimasuka?

- はい、ちゅーりっぷが窓辺の上にあります。
-hai, chu-rippu ga madobe no ue ni arimasu.

- 本は部屋にありますか？
-hon ha heya ni arimasuka?

- はい、沢山の本が本棚の中にあります。
-hai, takusan no hon ga hondana no naka ni arimasu.

- 本棚はどこですか？
-hondana ha doko desuka?

- picture. It is big and beautiful.

- What is there on the mantelpiece?

- There is a photo and a vase on the mantelpiece.

- What is in the vase?

- There are beautiful yellow roses in the vase.

- How many roses are there in the vase?

- There are six roses in the vase.

- Are there more flowers in this room?

- Yes, there are tulips on the windowsill.

- Are there books in this room?

- Yes, there are a lot of books in the bookcase.

- Where is the bookcase?

- It is located near the

- どあの 近くにあります。
-doa no chikaku ni arimasu.
- 本棚の中には何がありますか？
-hondana no naka niha nani ga arimasuka?
- 本棚の中には本と写真があります。
- hondana no naka ni ha hon to shashin ga arimasu.
- しぇいくすぴあの本は本棚にありますか？
-sheikusupia no hon ha hondana ni arimasuka?
- はい、それらは赤です。
-hai, soreraha aka desu.
- 本棚の中には棚がいくつありますか？
-hondana no naka ni ha tana ga ikutsu arimasuka?
- 本棚の中には棚が4つあります。
-hondana no naka niha tana ga yottsu arimasu.
- 天井には何がありますか？
-tenjou niha nani ga arimasuka?
- 天井には新しいしゃんでりあがあります。
-tenjou niha atarashii shanderia ga arimasu.
-スイッチはどこですか？
-suicchi ha doko desuka?
-すいっちは壁の右にあります。
-suicchi ha kabe no migi ni arimasu.
-この部屋にはもっとらんぷがありますか？
-kono heya niha motto ranpu ga arimasuka?
-そふぁーの近くにもう1つらんぷがあります。
-sofa no chikaku ni mou hitotsu ranpu ga arimasu.

- door.
- What is there in the bookcase?
- There are books and photographs in the bookcase.
- Are there books by Shakepseare in the bookcase?
- Yes, they are red.
- How many shelves are there in the bookcase?
- In the bookcase there are four shelves.
- What is there on the ceiling?
- There is a new chandelier on the ceiling.
- Where's the switch?
- The switch is on the wall on the right.
- Are there more lamps in the room?
- There is another

-らんぷは何色ですか？
-ranpu ha naniiro desuka?
-それはベージュです。
-sore ha be-ju desu.
-あなたはてれびを持っていますか？
-anata ha terebi wo motteimasuka?
-はい、それは角にあります。
-hai, sore ha kado ni arimasu.
-てれびは大きいですかそれとも小さいですか？
-terebi ha ookii desuka soretomo chiisai desuka?
-それは大きくて黒いです。
-sore ha ookikute kuroi desu.
-このらじおは機能しますか？
-kono rajio ha kinou shimasuka?
-はい、それは機能します。
-hai, sore ha kinou shimasu.

lamp near the sofa.

- What color is this lamp?

- It is beige.

- Do you have a TV?

- Yes, it is in the corner.

- Is the TV big or small?

- It's big and black.

- Does this radio work?

- Yes, it works.

4

Audio

氷(こおり)を砕(くだ)く
Break the ice

お父(とう)さんと娘(むすめ)は公園(こうえん)から帰宅(きたく)しました。娘(むすめ)は公園(こうえん)に戻(もど)って遊(あそ)びたいらしく。駄々(だだ)をこね始(はじ)めたのです。

"どうしたの？"とお母(かあ)さんは娘(むすめ)に聞(き)くと。"ぱぱがね…子供(こども)たちをいじめているんだ！"と娘(むすめ)は叫(さけ)んだのです。

A dad and his little daughter return home from the playground. The daughter wants to go back to the playground and continue playing. She begins to cry.

"What happened?" the mom asks.

"This daddy ... our daddy is torturing children!" the little girl shouts.

"子供たち？"とお母さんは言いいました。

"私よ！"

"What children?" the mom asks.

"Me!" the daughter responds.

otōsan to musume wa kōen kara kitakushimashita. musume wa kōen ni modotte asobitai rashiku. dada o konehajimeta no desu. dō shita no? to okāsan wa musume ni kiku to. papa ga ne kodomotachi o ijimeteiru n da! to musume wa sakenda no desu. kodomotachi? to okāsan wa iiimashita. watashi yo!

バスルーム
The bathroom

A

単語
Words

1. (シャワーを)浴びる、(薬を)飲む [(shawa- wo) abiru, (kusuri wo) nomu] - take (a shower, medicine etc.)
2. 〜と一緒に [〜to isshoni] - with
3. 〜を聞く [〜wo kiku] - listen to
4. きれい [kirei] - clean
5. の隣に、近く [no tonarini, chikaku] - next to, near
6. ゴミ、生ごみ [gomi, namagomi] - trash, garbage
7. シャワー [shawa-] - shower
8. タオル [taoru] - towel

9. トイレ、バスルーム [toire, basuru-mu] - toilet, bathroom
10. バスケット [basuketto] - basket
11. バスタブ [basutabu] - bathtub
12. バスルーム [basuru-mu] - bathroom
13. ブラシ [burashi] - brush
14. 可能な、できる [kanouna, dekiru] - possible
15. 機械 [kikai] - machine
16. 休む、リラックス [yasumu, rirakkusu] - rest, relax
17. 作る [tsukuru] - make
18. 紙 [kami] - paper
19. 歯 [ha] - teeth, tooth
20. 自分の体を洗う [jibunno karada wo arau] - wash oneself
21. 蛇口、栓 [jaguchi, sen] - faucet, tap
22. 取っ手 [totte] - handle
23. 小さいラグ、マット [chiisairagu, matto] - little rug, mat
24. 食べる [taberu] - eat
25. 食べ物 [tabemono] - food
26. 石鹸 [sekken] - soap
27. 洗う、きれいにする [arau, kireinisuru] - wash, clean
28. 洗濯、洗う [sentaku, arau] - washing
29. 洗濯物、下着、リネン [sentakumono, shitagi, rinen] - laundry, underwear, linen
30. 洗面台 [senmendai] - washbasin
31. 読む [yomu] - read
32. 熱い [atsui] - hot
33. 用意する、料理する [youisuru, ryourisuru] - prepare, cook
34. 冷たい、寒い [tsumetai, samui] - cold
35. 話す、喋る [hanasu, shaberu] - talk, chat

B

私たちはばするーむへ移動します。ばするーむは小さくて明るいです。ばするーむの中の壁は青です。天井は白です。

watashitachi ha basuru-mu he idou shimasu. basuru-mu ha chiisakute akarui desu. basuru-mu no naka no kabe ha ao desu. tenjou ha shiro desu.

-これは何ですか？

-kore ha nan desuka?

-これはばすたぶです。

-kore ha basutabu desu.

We proceed to the bathroom. The bathroom is small and bright. The walls in the bathroom are blue. The ceiling is white.

- What is this?

- This is the bathtub.

—それはぷらすちっくですかまたは金属ですか？
-sore ha purasuchikku desuka mataha kinzoku desuka?
-そのタブはプラスチックです。
-sono tabu ha purasuchikku desu.
—ばすたぶの上には何がありますか？
-basutabu no ue niha nani ga arimasuka?
—これは蛇口としゃわーです。熱い水の栓と冷たい水の栓があります。
-kore ha jaguchi to shawa- desu. atsui mizu no sen to tsumetai mizu no sen ga arimasu.
—壁には何がかけてありますか？
- kabe ni ha nani ga kakete arimasuka?
—これはきれいなたおるです。それは青です。
-kore ha kirei na taoru desu. sore ha ao desu.
—ばすたぶの近くの床には何が横たわっていますか？
- basutabu no chikaku no yuka ni ha nani ga yokotawatte imasuka?
—まっとがばすたぶの近くに横たわっています。
-matto ga basutabu no chikaku ni yokotawatte imasu.
—その右には何がありますか？
-sono migi niha nani ga arimasuka?
—これは洗面台です。鏡が洗面台の上にかけてあります。そこには熱い水と冷たい水の栓もあります。
-koreha senmendai desu. kagami ga senmendai no ue ni kakete arimasu. soko niha atsui mizu to tsumetai mizu no sen mo arimasu.

- Is it plastic or metal?

- The tub is plastic.

- What is there above the bathtub?

- This is a faucet and shower. There is a tap with hot water and a tap with cold water.

- What is hanging on the wall?

- This is a clean towel. It is blue.

- What is lying near the bathtub on the floor?

- A mat is lying near the bathtub.

- What is there on the right?

- This is a washbasin. There is a mirror hanging over the washbasin. There is also a tap with hot

-しんくの上には何がありますか？
-shinku no ue niha nani ga arimasuka?
-しんくの上には石鹸と歯ぶらしがあります。
-shinku no ue ni ha, sekken to haburashi ga arimasu.
-しんくの近くには何がありますか？
- shinku no chikaku ni ha nani ga arimasuka?
-それは洗濯機です。それは白です。その洗濯機は新しいです。
-sore ha sentakki desu. sore ha shiro desu. Sono sentakki ha atarashii desu.
-洗濯機の近くには何がありますか？
-sentakki no chikaku niha nani ga arimasuka?
-汚い洗濯物のためのばすけっとが洗濯機の近くにあります。
-kitanai sentakki no tameno basuketto ga sentakki no chikaku ni arimasu.
-角には何がありますか？
- kado ni ha nani ga arimasuka?
-ごみ箱が角にあります。
-gomibako ga kado ni arimasu.
-洗面台の後ろには何がありますか？
- senmendai no ushiro ni ha nani ga arimasuka?
-といれが洗面台の後ろにあります。
-toire ga senmendai no ushiro ni arimasu.
-便器の近くには何がありますか？

and cold water.

- What is there on the sink?

- On the sink, there are soap and toothbrushes.

- What is near the sink?

- It is a washing machine. It is white. The washing machine is new.

- What is there near the washing machine?

- There is a basket for dirty laundry near the washing machine.

- What is there in the corner?

- There is a trash can in the corner.

- What is behind the wash basin?

- There is a toilet

- benki no chikaku ni ha nani ga arimasuka?
-これはトイレットペーパーとトイレブラシです。
-kore ha toirettope-pa- soshite toireburashi desu.
-ばするーむの 中 では 何 ができますか？
-basuru-mu no naka de ha nani ga dekimasuka?
-ばするーむの 中 では、あなたは手を 洗ったり、体を 洗ったり、お風呂に 入ったり、そして歯を 磨くことができます。
-basuru-mu no naka deha, anata ha te wo arattari, karada wo arattari, ofuro ni haittari, soshite ha wo migaku koto ga dekimasu.
-きっちんの 中 では 何 ができますか？
- kicchin no naka de ha nani ga dekimasuka?
-きっちんの 中 では、あなたは食べ物を 料理したり、そして食器を 洗うことができます。
-kicchin no naka de ha, anata ha tabemono wo ryouri shitari, soshite shokki wo arau koto ga dekimasu.
-だいにんぐるーむの 中 では 何 ができますか？
-daininguru-mu no naka de ha nani ga dekimasuka?
-だいにんぐるーむの 中 では、あなたは料理を食べたり、そして話をすることができます。
-daininguru-mu no naka de ha, anata ha ryouri wo tabetari, soshite hanashi wo suru koto ga dekimasu.
-りびんぐるーむの 中 では 何 ができますか？
- ribinguru-mu no naka de ha nani ga dekimasuka?
-りびんぐるーむの 中 では、あなたはりらっくすしたり、て

behind the washbasin.

- What is near the toilet bowl?

- This is toilet paper and a toilet brush.

- What can you do in the bathroom?

- In the bathroom you can wash your hands, wash, bath, and brush your teeth.

- What can you do in the kitchen?

- In the kitchen you can cook food and wash dishes.

- What can you do in the dining room?

- In the dining room, you can eat and talk.

- What can you do in the living room?

- In the living room, you can relax, watch

れびを見たり、らじおを聴いたり、話をしたり、そして読むことができます。

-ribinguru-mu no naka de ha, anata ha rirakkusu shitari, terebi wo mitari, rajio wo kiitari, hanashi wo shitari, soshite yomu koto ga dekimasu.

TV, listen to the radio, talk, read.

5

Audio

氷を砕く
Break the ice

"あなたのくらすには何人女の子がいるの?"とお母さんは娘に聞きました。

"七人いるよ"と娘は答えます。

"男の子は?"とお母さんが聞くと。

"いっぱいいるけど、いつも走り回ってるから数えるのは無理だよ"と答えました。

"How many girls are there in your class?" a mom asks her little daughter.

"There are seven girls in the class," the girl answers.

"What about the boys?" the mom asks.

"There is a lot of the boys. But they always run back and forth. It is impossible to count them," the girl answers.

anata no kurasu ni wa nan nin onnanoko ga iru no? to okāsan wa musume ni kikimashita. nana nin iru yo to musume wa kotaemasu. otokonoko wa? to okāsan ga kiku to.ippai iru kedo, itsumo hashirimawatteru kara kazoeru no wa muri da yo to kotaemashita.

あなたはドイツ語またはスペイン語を話せますか？
Can you speak German or Spanish?

A

単語
Words

1. (電話を)かける [(denwa wo)kakeru] - call (by phone)
2. 〜である [〜de aru] - be
3. 〜の後 [〜no ato] - after
4. あなた [anata] - you
5. あなたの [anatano] - your(s)
6. おそらく [osoraku] - probably
7. かもしれない [kamoshirenai] - maybe
8. きれいにする、かたづける [kireinisuru, katazukeru] - clean, tidy up
9. しかし、けれども [shikashi, keredomo] - but
10. しなければならない、せざるをえない [shinakerebanaranai, sezaruwoenai] - have to, be obliged
11. できる、することができる [dekiru, surukotoga dekiru] - be able to, can
12. なぜ、どうして [naze, doushite] - why
13. カフェ [kafe] - cafe
14. コンピューター [konpyu-ta-] - computer
15. ノートブック [notobukku] - notebook, copybook
16. バスケットボール [basukettobo-ru] - basketball
17. フランス語 [furansugo] - French

18. 一生懸命働く [isshoukenmei hataraku] - work hard
19. 映画館 [eigakan] - cinema, movie theater
20. 英語 [eigo] - English
21. 家へ帰る道 [ie he kaerumichi] - homeward
22. 教える [oshieru] - teach
23. 兄弟 [kyoudai] - brother
24. 言語/言葉 [gengo/ kotoba] - language / tongue
25. 行く、散歩をする、歩く [iku, sanpo wo suru, aruku] - go, walk
26. 今 [ima] - now
27. 今日 [kyou] - today
28. 私 [watashi] - I
29. 私たちの [watashitachino] - our(s)
30. 私の [watashino] - my
31. 取る [toru] - take
32. 書く [kaku] - write
33. 助ける、手伝う [tasukeru, tetsudau] - help
34. 少し、少量の [sukoshi, suuryouno] - a bit, a little
35. 他の [hokano] - other
36. 待つ [motsu] - wait
37. 置く [oku] - put (down)
38. 喋る [shaberu] - speak
39. 店 [mise] - store, shop
40. 電話する [denwasuru] - phone
41. 働く、仕事 [hataraku, shigoto] - work
42. 彼に、彼を、彼の [kareni, karewo, kareno] - him, his
43. 必要がある、しなければならない [hitsuyouga aru, shinakerebanaranai] - be necessary, need to
44. 病気になる [byoukininaru] - get sick
45. 名前で呼ぶ、名前をつける [namaede yobu, namae wo tsukeru] - call, name
46. 明日 [ashita] - tomorrow
47. 木 [ki] - tree
48. 夜に [yoruni] - in the evening
49. 友達 [tomodachi] - friend
50. 遊ぶ [asobu] - play
51. 良い、上手い [yoi, umai] - well

B

1

-あなたは英語またはふらんす語を読むことができますか？
-anata ha eigo mataha furansugo wo yomukoto ga dekimasuka?
- 私は英語とふらんす語の読み書きができます。
-watashi ha eigo to furansugo no yomi kaki ga dekimasu.
-これらの言語を喋れますか？

1

- Can you read in English or in French?

- I can read and write in English and in

-korera no gengo wo shaberemasuka?

- 私は英語を少し話せます。私はふらんす語は話しません。

-watashi ha eigo wo sukoshi hanase masu. Watashi ha furansugo ha hanashimasen.

-あなたはどいつ語またはすぺいん語を喋ることができますか？

-anata ha doitsugo mataha supeingo wo shaberukoto ga dekimasuka?

-はい、私はどいつ語とすぺいん語を上手く話せます。

-hai, watashi ha doitsugo to supeingo wo umaku hanasemasu.

-すぺいん語の喋り方を私に教えてくれますか？

-supeingo no shaberikat wo oshiete kuremasuka?

-はい、教えれますよ。しかしあなたは頑張って勉強しないといけません。

-hai, oshieremasuyo. shikashi anata ha ganbatte benkyou shinaito ikemasen.

2

-あなたはバスケットボールはできますか？

-basukettobo-ru ha dekimasuka?

-いいえ、けれども私はそれを学ぶことはできます。

-iie, keredomo watashi ha sore wo manabukoto ha dekimasu.

-明日試合をするのはどうですか？

-ashita shiai wo suruno ha doudesuka?

-明日はできませんが、今日はできます。

-ashita ha dekimasen ga, kyou ha dekimasu.

-それなら今夜はどうですか？

-sorenara konya ha doudesuka?

-はい、私は夜には試合ができます。あなたの

- Can you speak these languages?

- I can speak a little English. I do not speak French.

- Can you speak German or Spanish?

- Yes, I speak German and Spanish well.

- Can you teach me how to speak Spanish?

- Yes, I can. But you have to work.

2

- Can you play basketball?

- No, but I can learn.

- Maybe we'll play tomorrow?

- I can't tomorrow, but today I can.

- Maybe tonight?

- Yes, I can play in the

ともだち　よ
友達を呼べますか？
-hai, watashi ha yoru niha shiai ga dekimasu. anata no tomocachi wo yobemasuka?
　　　よ
-はい、呼べます。
-hai, yobemasu.

3

　　　　あに
-あなたの兄どこですか？
-anata no ani ha dokodesuka?
わたし　　　かれ　ま
-私たちは彼を待たなければいけません。
-watashitachi ha kare wo matanakereba narimasen.
かれ　　　　　き　　　　かえ
-彼はおそらく来ません。帰ってもいいですか？
-kare ha osoraku kimasen. kaettemo iidesuka?
　　　かえ
-はい、帰ってもいいです。
-hai, kaettemo iidesu.

4

ほん　　も　い
-この本を持って行ってもいいですか？
-kono hon wo motte itte mo iidesuka?
　　　　ほん　　も　い
-いいえ、この本を持って行ってはいけません。
-iie, kono hon wo motte itte ha ikemasen.
　　　　　　　も　い
-このこっぷを持って行ってもいいですか？
-kono koppu wo motte itte mo iidesuka?
　　　　　　　　　　　　も　い
-いいえ、このこっぷを持って行ってはいけません。きっ
　　　　　た　　　も　い
ちんから他のこっぷを持って行ってもいいですよ。
-iie, kono koppu wo motte itte ha ikemasen. kicchin kara hoka no koppu wo motte itte mo iidesuyo.
　　　　ともだち
-あなたの友達はどこですか？
-anata no tomodachi ha dokodesuka?
かれ　　　　　　そと
-彼はおそらく外です。
-kare ha osoraku soto desu.

evening. Can you call your friends?

- Yes, I can.

3

- Where is your brother?

- We have to wait for him.

- He probably will not come. Can I go home?

- Yes, you can.

4

- Can I take this book?

- No, you may not take this book.

- Can I take this cup?

- No, you may not take this cup. You can take another cup from the kitchen.

- Where is your friend?

- He's probably outside.

5

- 私はおそらく映画を観に行きます。あなたは私と一緒に来れますか？
-watashi ha osoraku eiga wo mini iki masu. anata ha watashi to issho ni koremasuka?

-いいえ、行けません。私は仕事をしなければいけません。
-iie, ikemasen. watashi ha shigoto wo shinakereba ikemasen.

-あなたは仕事の後には行けますか？
-anata ha shigoto no ato niha ikemasuka?

-はい、仕事の後には行くことができます。
-hai, shigoto no ato iku koto ga dekimasu.

- 私の本はどこですか？
-watashi no hon ha doko desuka?

-おそらくそれは本棚の中にあります。
-osoraku hondana no naka ni arimasu.

-あなたのぺんを持って行ってもいいですか？
-anata no pen wo motte ittemo iidesuka?

-はい、本棚からぺんを持って行ってもいいです。
-hai, hondana kara pen wo motte ittemo iidesu.

6

-こののーとぶっくを持って行ってもいいですか？
-kono no-tobukku wo motte ittemo iidesuka?

-いいえ、こののーとぶっくを持って行ってはいけません。
-iie, kono no-tobukku wo motte itteha ikemasen.

-てーぶるに着いてもいいですか？
-te-buru ni suwattemo iidesuka?

-はい、着いてもいいです。
-hai, suwattemo iidesu.

5

- I'll probably go to the movies. Can you come with me?

- No, I can't. I have to do work.

- Maybe you go after work?

- Yes, I can go after work.

- Where is my book?

- It's probably in the bookcase.

- Can I take your pen?

- Yes, you can take a pen from the bookcase.

6

- Can I take this notebook?

- No, you may not take this notebook.

- Can I sit down at the table?

- Yes, you can.

- 私ののーとぶっくをここに置いてもいいですか？
-watashi no no-tobukku wo koko ni oitemo iidesuka?

-はい、置いてもいいです。
-hai, oitemo iidesu.

-そのこんぴゅーたーで遊んでもいいですか？
-sono konpyu-ta- de asondemo iidesuka?

-はい、今遊んでもいいです。
-hai, ima asondemo iidesu.

-私は電話をしなければいけません。この電話を持って行ってもいいですか？
-watashi ha denwa wo shinakereba narimasen. kono denwa wo motte ittemo iidesuka?

-はい、持って行ってもいいです。
-hai, motte ittemo iidesu.

-一緒にかふぇに行けますか？
-issho ni kafe ni itkemasuka?

-いいえ、私は仕事に行かなければいけません。
-iie, watashi ha shigoto ni ikanakereba ikemasen.

7

-私たちのねこはどこですか？
-watashitachi no neko ha doko desuka?

-彼はおそらく木の中です。
-kare ha osoraku ki no naka desu.

-もしかしたら彼は家にいるかもしれませんか？
-moshikashitara kare ha ie ni iru kamo shiremasenka?

-いいえ、彼は家の中にはいません。
-iie, kare ha ie no naka niha imasen.

8

-どうしてあなたの友達は来なかったのですか？
-doushite anata no tomodachi ha konakatta nodesuka?

- Can I put my notebook here?
- Yes, you can.
- Can I play on the computer?
- Yes, you can play now.
- I need to make a phone call. Can I take this phone?
- Yes, you can take it.
- Can we go to the cafe?
- No, I have to go to work.

7

- Where is our cat?
- He's probably in the tree.
- Maybe he's in the house?
- No, he is not in the house.

8

- Why did your friend

- 彼はおそらく病気です。
-kare ha osoraku byouki desu.
- あなたは今りびんぐるーむをきれいにする必要があります。
-anata ha ima ribinguru-mu wo kirei ni suru hitsuyou ga arimasu.
- あなたは手伝ってくれますか？
-anata ha tetsudatte kuremasuka?
- いいえ、私は食器を洗わなければいけません。
-iie, watashi ha shokki wo arawanakereba ikemasen.

9

- 歯ぶらしはどこですか？
-haburashi ha dokodesuka?
- それらは洗濯機の上にあるかもしれません。
-sorera ha sentakki no ue ni arukamo shiremasen.
- 私の赤いのーとぶっくはどこですか？
-watashi no akai no-tobukku ha dokodesuka?
- それはおそらくかうちの上にあります。
-sore ha osoraku kauchi no ue ni arimasu.
- あなたは私と一緒に店まで来てくれますか？
-anata ha watashi to issho ni mise made kite kuremasuka?
- はい、私は行けます。
-hai, watashi ha ikemasu.

not come?
- He's probably sick.
- You have to clean the living room now.
- Maybe you will help me?
- No, I have to wash the dishes.

9

- Where are the toothbrushes?
- Maybe they are on the washing machine.
- Where is my red notebook?
- It's probably on the couch.
- Maybe you'll come with me to the store?
- Yes, I can go.

6

Audio

氷を砕く
Break the ice

お父(とう)さんはたまに、幼(おさな)い娘(むすめ)のためにしんでれらを読(よ)んであげます。
"私(わたし)の事(こと)を愛(あい)してくれる人(ひと)なんか現(あらわ)れないのだわ"とお父(とう)さんは読(よ)み上(あ)げました。娘(むすめ)はお父(とう)さんから本(ほん)を取(と)り上(あ)げてこう言(い)いました。
"現(あらわ)れるわよ！"と娘(むすめ)は言(い)い、本(ほん)をひっくり返(かえ)しながら"王子様(おうじさま)があなたのことを愛(あい)してくれるわ！"と言(い)ったのでした。

A dad sometimes reads the story of Cinderella to his little daughter. Today he is reading it again.

"I will never have somebody who loves me, Cinderella said and cried sadly," the dad reads aloud. The daughter quickly takes the book from his hands.

"You will! You will!" she says and flips through the book, "the prince will love you!"

otōsan wa tamani, osanai musume no tameni Shinderera o yondeagemasu. watashi no koto o aishitekureru hito nanka arawarenai no da wa to otōsan wa yomiagemashita. musume wa otōsan kara hon o toriagete kō iimashita. arawareru wa yo! to musume wa ii, hon o hikkurikaeshi nagara ōji sama ga anata no koto o aishitekureru wa! to itta no deshita.

助けてくれませんか？
Can you help me?

単語
Words

1. 5、五 [go, go] - five
2. しかし・けれども、〜の間、そして [shikashi, keredomo, 〜no aida, soshite] - but, while, and
3. すべて [subete] - all
4. そこ [soko] - there (place)
5. そして [soshite] - then
6. ねこ [neko] - cat
7. の上、に沿って [no ue, ni sotte] - over, along
8. もちろん [mochiron] - of course
9. やく [yaku] - about
10. イタリア人 [itariajin] - Italian (person)
11. ガレージ、車庫 [gare-ji, shako] - garage
12. コレクション [korekushon] - collection
13. サッカー [sakka-] - soccer
14. スイッチを入れる [suicchi wo ireru] - turn on

15. スペイン人 [supeinjin] - Spaniard
16. ツアー客 [tsua-kyaku] - tourist
17. バイク、オートバイ [baiku, o-tobai] - motorcycle, motorbike
18. パパ [papa] - Dad
19. ママ [mama] - Mom
20. 愛、愛する、好き [ai, aisuru, suki] - love
21. 飲む [nomu] - drink
22. 何年 [nannen] - how many years
23. 眼鏡 [megane] - glasses
24. 牛乳 [gyuunyuu] - milk
25. 近所 [kinjo] - neighbor
26. 警察 [keisatsu] - police
27. 見つける [mitsukeru] - find
28. 見る [miru] - see
29. 好き、好む [suki, konomu] - like, appeal
30. 紅茶 [koucha] - tea
31. 行く/乗って行く [iku/ notteiku] - go/ride away
32. 姉妹 [shimai] - sister
33. 私の(私の物) [watashino (watashinomono)] - my (mine)
34. 持つ、所有する、飼う [motsu, shoyuusuru, kau] - have, own
35. 時間 [jikan] - time
36. 自由、タダ [jiyuu, tada] - free
37. 住む [sumu] - live
38. 書く [kaku] - write (down)
39. 女性 [josei] - woman
40. 少し、いくつか [sukoshi, ikutsuka] - little, few
41. 乗る [noru] - ride
42. 新しくない [atarashikunai] - not new
43. 数字、番号 [suuji, bangou] - number
44. 誰 [dare] - who
45. 誰の [dareno] - whose
46. 探偵 [tantei] - detective
47. 男性 [dansei] - man
48. 電話 [denwa] - telephone
49. 年 [toshi] - year
50. 歩く、行く [aruku, iku] - walk, go
51. 冒険 [bouken] - adventure
52. 明かり、電気 [akari, denki] - light
53. 洋服、ローブ [youfuku, ro-bu] - clothing, robe

B

1

-あなたののーとぶっくを 持(もい)って行ってもいいですか？
-no-tobukku wo motte ittemo iidesuka?

-はい、持(もい)って行ってもいいです。それはてーぶるの上(うえ)にあります。私(わたし)ののーとぶっくは 青(あお)です。
-hai, motte ittemo iidesu. sore ha te-buru no ue ni arimasu.

1

- Can I take your notebook?

- Yes, you can. It is on the table. My notebook is

watashi no no-tobukku ha ao desu.

私 はそれを見つけることができません。
-watashi ha mitsukeru koto ga dekimasen.

私 ののーとぶっくはかうちの 上 にあるかもしれません。
-watashi no no-tobukku ha kauchi no ue ni aru kamo shiremasen.

-はい、それはかうちの 上 にあります。
-hai, sore ha kauchi no ue ni arimasu.

-あなたはもう１つぺんを持っていますか？ 私 は電話番号を書きとめる必要があります。
-anata ha mou hitotsu pen wo motte imasuka? watashi ha denwabangou wo kakitomeru hitsuyou ga arimasu.

私 のぺんはてーぶるの 上 にあります。それは金属です。
-watashi no pen ha te-buru no ue ni arimasu. sore ha kinzoku desu.

- blue.
- I cannot find it.
- Maybe my notebook is on the couch.
- Yes, it's on the couch.
- Do you have another pen? I need to write down a phone number.
- My pen is on the table. It's metal.

2

-あなたのねこは何才ですか？
-anata no neko ha nansai desuka?

私 たちのねこは５才です。
-watashitachi no neko ha gosai desu.

-あなたのねこは何を食べるのが好きですか？
-anata no neko ha nani wo taberuno ga suki desuka?

私 たちのねこは牛乳を飲むのが好きです。
-watashitachi no neko ha gyunyu wo nomuno ga suki desu.

彼女のねこは何才ですか？
-kanojo no neko ha nansai desuka?

彼女のねこは３才です。
-kanojo no neko ha sansai desu.

2

- How old is your cat?
- Our cat is five years old.
- What does your cat like to eat?
- Our cat likes to drink milk.
- How old is her cat?
- Her cat is three years old.

- あなたには沢山友達がいますか？
-anata niha takusan tomodachi ga imasuka?
- はい、私には沢山友達がいます。
-hai, watashi niha takusan tomodachi ga imasu.
- 私はこの町の中に友達がいません。
-watashi ha kono machi no naka ni tomodachi ga imasen.
- 私たちは夜に私の友達と一緒に映画に行くかもしれません。あなたは私たちと一緒に来れますか？
-watashitachi ha yoru ni watashi no tomodachi to issho ni eiga ni ikukamo shiremasen. anata ha watashitachi to issho ni koremasuka?
- はい、行けます。
-hai, ikemasu.
- あなたの姉は私たちと一緒に来れますか？
-anata no ane ha watashitachi to issho ni koremasuka?
- 私は彼女に電話できます。
-watashiha kanojo ni denwa dekimasu.
- 私は夜にあなたに電話します。
-watashi ha yoruni anata ni denwa shimasu.
- あなたの友達はこの町に住んでいますか？
-anata no tomodachi ha kono machi no naka ni sunde imasuka?
- はい、私の友達はみんなこの町に住んでいます。
-hai, watashi no tomodachi ha minna kono machi ni sundeimasu.

- Do you have many friends?

- Yes, I have many friends.

- I have no friends in this town.

- Maybe in the evening we will go to the movies with my friends. Can you come with us?

- Yes, I can.

- Will your sister go with us?

- I can call her.

- I'll call you in the evening.

- Do your friends live in this city?

- Yes, all of my friends live in this city.

4

- 私は部屋をきれいにしなければなりません。手伝ってくれませんか？
-watashi ha heya wo kireini shinakereba narimasen. tetsudatte kuremasenka?
-いいえ、私は私の電話を探さないといけません。
-iie, watashi ha watashi no denwa wo sagasanaito ikemasen.
-あなたの電話はきっちんにあるかもしれません。
-anata no denwa ha kicchin ni arukamo shiremasen.
-私の電話を探すのを手伝ってください、そしたら私はあなたが部屋をきれいにするのを手伝います。
-watashi no denwa wo sagasuno wo tetsudatte kudasai. Soshitara watashi ha anata ga heya wo kirei ni suruno wo tetsudaimasu.

5

-あなたは何か面白い本は持っていませんか？
-anata ha nani ga omoshiroi hon ha motte imasenka?
-私は本のこれくしょんを沢山持っています。多くの本は冒険についてです。愛についての本もあります。
-watashi ha hon no korekushon wo takusan motte imasu. ooku no hon ha bouken ni tsuite desu. ai ni tsuiteno hon mo arimasu.
-あなたは探偵の本を持っていますか？
-anata ha tantei no hon wo motte imasuka?
-いくつかあります。
-ikutsuka arimasu.
-それらを見てもいいですか？
-sorera wo mitemo iidesuka?

4

- I have to clean the room. Can you help me?
- No, I need to find my phone.
- Perhaps your phone is in the kitchen.
- Help me find my phone, and I'll help you clean the room.

5

- Do you have any interesting books?
- I have a large collection of books. Many of them are about adventures. There are also books about love.
- Do you have detective books?
- A few.
- Can I see them?
- Yes, you can. They are

-はい、見てもいいです。それらは本棚の上にあります。棚の右側の上にあります。
-hai, mitemo iidesu. Sorera ha hondana no ue ni arimasu. tana no migigawa no ue ni arimasu.
-私のお母さんも本のこれくしょんを持っています。
-watashi no okaasan mo hon no korekushon wo motte imasu.

- on the bookshelf. On the shelf on the right.
- My mother also has a collection of books.

6

-私はぱぱの眼鏡を探す必要があります。それらはどこですか？
-watashi ha papa no megane wo sagasu hitsuyou ga arimasu. sorera ha dokodesuka?
-彼の眼鏡は棚の上にあるかもしれません。
-kare no megane ha tana no ue ni arukamo shiremasen.
-いいえ、彼の眼鏡はそこにはありません。
-iie, kare no megane ha sokoniha arimasen.
-そしたらそれは部屋の中のてーぶるの上にあります。
-soshitara sore ha heya no naka no te-buru no ue ni arimasu.
-彼の眼鏡を見つけました。
-kare no megane wo mitsuke mashita.

6

- I need to find Dad's glasses. Where are they?
- Maybe his glasses are on the shelf.
- No, his glasses are not there.
- Then they are in the room on the table.
- I found his glasses.

7

-私は私たちのこっぷを洗う必要があります。
-watashi ha watashitachi no koppu wo arau hitsuyou ga arimasu.
-あなたはこっぷを今洗わなければいけませんか？
-anata ha koppu wo ima arawanakereba ikemasenka?
-はい、私はそれらを今洗わなければなりません。
-hai, watashi ha sorera wo ima arawanakereba narimasen.

7

- I have to wash our cups.
- You have to wash the cups now?
- Yes, I have to wash them now.

- この部屋の中にきれいなこっぷはありますか？
-kono heya no naka ni kireina koppu ha arimasuka?
- はい、そこの棚の上に沢山きれいなこっぷがあります。
-hai, soko no tana no ue ni takusan kireina koppu ga arimasu.
- どのこっぷが私のですか？
-dono koppu ga watashi no desuka?
- あなたのこっぷは黄色、しかし私のは青です。
-anatano koppu ha kiiro, shikashi watashino ha ao desu.

8

- この男性は私のぱぱです。これはぱぱの家です。
-kono dansei ha watashi no papa desu. kore ha papa no ie desu.
- 彼の家は新しいですか？
-kare no ie ha atarashii desuka?
- いいえ、彼の家は新しくありません。
-iie, kare no ie ha atarashiku arimasen.
- これはあなたの車ですか？
-kore ha anata no kuruma desuka?
- いいえ、この車は青です、そして私たちの車は赤です。
-iie, kono kuruma ha ao desu, soshite watashitachi no kuruma ha aka desu.

9

- これは私のままです。
-kore ha watashi no mama desu.
- 彼女は出て行くところですか？
-kanojo ha deteiku tokoro desuka?
- はい、彼女は仕事に行きます。
-hai, kanojo ha shigoto ni ikimasu.

- Are there clean cups in this room?

- Yes, there are many clean cups on that shelf.

- Which cup is mine?

- Your cup is yellow, but mine is blue.

8

- This man is my dad. This is Dad's home.

- Is his house new?

- No, his house is not new.

- Is this your car?

- No, this is a blue car, and our car is red.

9

- This is my mom.

- Is she leaving?

- Yes, she is going to work.

- Is this her car?

-これは彼女の車ですか？
-kore ha kanojo no kuruma desuka?
-はい、これは私のお母さんの車です。彼女の車は新しいです。
-hai, kore ha watashi no okaasan no kuruma desu. kanojo no kuruma ha atarashii desu.
-あなたのぱぱも車を持っていますか？
-anata no papa mo kuruma wo mochimasuka?
-はい、彼の車はがれーじの中にあります。
-hai, kare no kuruma ha gare-ji no naka ni arimasu.

- Yes, this is my mother's car. Her car is new.
- Does your dad also have a car?
- Yes, his car is in the garage.

10

-あなたは犬が好きですか？
-anata ha inu ga suki desuka?
-いいえ、しかし私のままは犬を飼っています。
-iie, shikashi watashi no mama ha inu wo katte imasu.
-この犬があなたのままの犬ですか？
-kono inu ga anata no mama no inu desuka?
-はい、この犬が彼女の犬です。
-hai, kono inu ga kanojo no inu desu.

- Do you like dogs?
- No, but my mom has a dog.
- This dog is your mother's?
- Yes, it is her dog.

11

-あなたの部屋はどこですか？
-anata no heya ha doko desuka?
-私の部屋は右にあります。そこはきれいで明るいです。
-watashi no heya ha migi ni arimasu. soko ha kirei de akarui desu.
-左には誰の部屋がありますか？
-hidari niha dare no heya ga arimasuka?
-これはお母さんの部屋です。彼女の部屋は大きくて美しいです。

11

- Where is your room?
- My room on the right. It is clean and bright.
- Whose room is on the left?
- This is my mother's room. Her room is big

-kore ha okaasan no heya desu. kanojo no heya ha ookikute utsukushii desu.

12

-けとるの 中に 水 はありますか？
-ketoru no naka ni mizu ha arimasuka?
-はい、けとるの 中 には 水 が 少 しあります。
-hai, ketoru no naka niha mizu ga sukoshi arimasu.
- 紅 茶 をもらってもいいですか？
-koucha wo morattemo iidesuka?
-はい、もちろん。
-hai, mochiron.

13

- 私 たちのねこは 牛 乳 を 少 ししか飲みませんでした。
-watashitachi no neko ha gyunyu wo sukoshi shika nomimasen deshita.
- 私 は彼 女 は病 気 だったと思 います。
-watashi ha kanojo ha byouki dattato omoi masu.

14

-この 町 には 沢 山 のいたりあ 人 とすぺいん人はいますか？
-kono machi niha takusan no itariajin to supeinjin ha imasuka?
-はい、沢 山 のつあー 客 がいます。
-hai, takusan no tsua-kyaku ga imasu.
- 私 たちの 町 は 美 しいです。
-watashitachi no machi ha utsukushii desu.
- 私 はここに住むのが好きです。
-watashi ha koko ni sumuno ga suki desu.

15

-その 人 は 誰 ですか？
-sonohito ha dare desuka?
-この 人 は 私 の 友 達 のろばーとです。

12

- Is there water in the kettle?

- Yes, there is a little water in the kettle.

- Can I have some tea?

- Yes, of course.

13

- Our cat drank just a little milk.

- I think she was ill.

14

- Are there many Italians and Spaniards in this city?

- Yes, there are a lot of tourists.

- Our city is beautiful.

- I like living here.

15

- Who's that?

- This is my friend Robert.

-konohito ha watashi no tomodachi no roba-to desu.
かれ ふく ふる
- 彼 の 服 は 古 いです。
-kare no fuku ha furui desu.
かれ か もの きら
- 彼 は 買 い 物 が 嫌 いです。
-kare ha kaimono ga kirai desu.

16

じょせい とお む がわ いえ す
-この 女 性 は 通 りの 向こう 側 の 家 に 住んでいますか？
-kono josei ha toori no mukougawa no ie ni sunde imasuka?
かのじょ わたし きんじょ
-はい、彼 女 は 私 たちのご 近 所 さんです。
-hai, kanojo ha watashitachi no gokinjosan desu.
かのじょ
-そこにあるのは 彼 女 のおーとばいですか？
-soko ni aruno ha kanojo no o-tobai desuka?
かのじょ
-はい、それは 彼 女 のおーとばいです。
-hai, sore ha kanojo no o-tobai desu.

17

へや あ すく でんき
-この部屋は、明かりが 少 ないです。電 気 をつけてくれますか？
-konoheya ha, akari ga sukunai desu. denki wo tsukete kuremasuka?
-はい、つけます。
-hai, tsuke masu.

18

きょうまち たくさん けいさつかん
- 今 日 町 には 沢 山 の 警 察 官 がいますか？
-kyou machi niha takusan no keisatsukan ga imasuka?
きょう しあい
-はい、今 日 はふっとぼーるの 試 合 です。
-hai, kyou ha futtobo-ru no shiai desu.
い
-ふっとぼーるまっちに行きませんか？
-futtobo-rumacchi ni ikimasenka?
わたし たくさん じゆうじかん
-はい、私 は 沢 山 の 自 由 時 間 があります。
-hai, watashi ha takusan no jiyujikan ga arimasu.

- His clothes are old.

- He does not like to shop.

16

- This woman lives in a house across the street?

- Yes, she is our neighbor.

- Is that her motorcycle there?

- Yes, it's her motorcycle.

17

- In this room, there is little light. Can you turn on the light?

- Yes, I can.

18

- Are there many policemen in the city today?

- Yes, today is the football game.

- Maybe we'll go to a football match?

- Yes, I have a lot of free time.

7

氷を砕く
Break the ice

誕生日会には沢山の子供たちが参加をしており、みんなでてーぶるを囲んでけーきを見ています。けーきの上にはちょこでできた動物が飾られています。

"誰かしまうま欲しい？"とお母さんは子供たちに聞きます。

"しまうまさんください"と女の子は言いました。

"お魚さんください"ともう一人の女の子が言いました。

There are many little children at a birthday party. They all sit at the table. A big cake is on the table. There are chocolate animals on the cake.

"Who wants the zebra?" the mom asks the children.

"Give me the zebra please," a girl says.

"Give me the fish please," another girl says.

"きりんさんください"と男の子が言いました。 "Give me the giraffe please," a boy says.

"すぷーんください"と別の男の子が言いました。 "Give me a spoon please," another boy says.

tanjōbikai ni wa takusan no kodomotachi ga sanka o shiteori, minna de te-buru o kakonde ke-ki o miteimasu. ke-ki no ueni wa choko de dekita dōbutsu ga kazarareteimasu. dare ka shimauma hoshii? to okāsan wa kodomotachi ni kikimasu. shimauma san kudasai to onnanoko wa iimashita. o sakana san kudasai to mō ichi nin no onnanoko ga iimashita. kirin san kudasai to otokonoko ga iimashita. supu-n kudasai to betsu no otokonoko ga iimashita.

あなたの名前は何ですか？
What's your name?

 A

単語
Words

1. 12、十二 [juuni, juuni] - twelve
2. 18、十八 [juuhachi, juuhachi] - eighteen
3. 1、一 [ichi, ichi] - one
4. 20、二十 [nijuu, nijuu] - twenty
5. 2、二 [ni, ni] - two
6. 40、四十 [yonjuu, yonjuu] - forty
7. 8、八 [hachi, hachi] - eight
8. 〜から、どこから [〜kara, dokokara] - from where
9. 〜へ [〜he] - to
10. 〜まで [〜made] - until, to

11. いくつか、いくらか [ikutsuka, ikuraka] - any, some
12. いつ [itsu] - when
13. いつも [itsumo] - always
14. お父さん [otousan] - father
15. こんにちは [konnichiwa] - hi, hello
16. そう遠くない昔、最近 [soutookunaimukashi, saikin] - not long ago, recently
17. とても [totemo] - very
18. どうやって [douyatte] - how
19. のどが渇く [nodoga kawaku] - thirty
20. よく [yoku] - often
21. イギリス [igirisu] - England
22. イギリスの女性 [igirisuno josei] - Englishwoman
23. イタリア [itaria] - Italy
24. クッキー [kukki-] - cookie
25. クラブ [kurabu] - club
26. ゲスト [gesuto] - guest
27. サーモン [sa-mon] - salmon
28. サッカー [sakka-] - soccer
29. サッカー選手 [sakka-senshu] - soccer player
30. スタンプ [sutanpu] - stamp
31. ドイツの [doitsuno] - German
32. ナポリ [napori] - Naples
33. ピザ [piza] - pizza
34. フランク [furanku] - Frank
35. メカニック [mekanikku] - mechanic
36. ライター、作家、記者 [raita-, sakka, kisha] - writer
37. 医者、医師 [isha, ishi] - doctor, physician
38. 育児室 [takujishitsu] - nursery
39. 英国 [eikoku] - Great Britain
40. 何年も [nannenmo] - years
41. 家、家庭 [ie, katei] - house/home
42. 家族 [kazoku] - family
43. 学校 [gakkou] - school
44. 寒い [samui] - cold
45. 休暇 [kyuuka] - vacation
46. 国 [kuni] - country
47. 国籍 [kokuseki] - nationality
48. 国民 [kokumin] - national
49. 皿 [sara] - dish
50. 産まれる [umareru] - be born
51. 子供 [kodomo] - child
52. 私たち [watashitachi] - us
53. 自動車、車 [jidousha, kuruma] - automobile, car
54. 車のサービス [kurumano sa-bisu] - car service
55. 修復、修理 [shuufuku, shuuri] - renovation, repairs
56. 乗る、行く [noru, iku] - ride, go
57. 職業、専門職 [shokugyou, senmonshoku] - profession
58. 人生 [jinsei] - life
59. 専門家、プロフェッショナル [senmonka, purofesshonaru] - professional
60. 全体、すべて [zentai, subete] - whole
61. 素晴らしい [subarashii] - excellent
62. 代理店、紹介所 [dairiten, shoukaijo] - agency
63. 大学 [daigaku] - university

64. 知り合いになる、習得する、習う [shiriaininaru, shuutokusuru, narau] - get acquainted, learn
65. 知る [shiru] - know
66. 動物 [doubutsu] - animal
67. 年上 [toshiue] - older
68. 売る [uru] - sell
69. 不動産 [fudousan] - real estate
70. 勉強する、学ぶ [benkyousuru, manabu] - study, learn
71. 郵便局 [yuubinkyoku] - post office
72. 旅行 [ryokou] - travel
73. 両親 [ryoushin] - parents

B

1

-こんにちは。
-konnichiha.

-こんにちは。あなたの名前は何ですか？
-konnichiha. anata no namae ha nan desuka?

-私の名前はふらんくです。そしてあなたの名前は何ですか？
-watashi no namae ha furanku desu. soshite anata no namae ha nan desuka?

-私の名前はまりおです。
-watashi no namae ha mario desu.

-あなたは何才ですか？
-anata ha nansai desuka?

-私は18才です。
-watashi ha juuhassai desu.

-あなたの国籍は何ですか？
-anata no kokuseki ha nan desuka?

-私は英国で生まれそして生活しています。私のぱぱはすぺいん人です。私のままはいぎりすの女性です。そしてあなたはどこから来ましたか？

1

- Hi.
- Hi. What's your name?
- My name is Frank. And what's your name?
- My name is Mario.
- How old are you?
- I'm eighteen years old.
- What is your nationality?
- I was born and live in Great Britain. My dad is a Spaniard. My mother is an Englishwoman. And where are you

-watashi ha eikoku de umare soshite seikatsushite imasu. watashi no papa ha supeinjin desu. watashi no mama ha igirisu no josei desu. soshite anata ha dokokara kimashitaka?

- 私はいたりあの国籍です。私はなぽりに住んでいます。あなたは働いていますか、もしくは勉強していますか？

-watashi ha itaria no kokuseki desu. watashi ha napori ni sunde imasu. anata ha hataraite imasuka, moshikuha benkyou shiteimasuka?

- 私はなしょなる大学の生徒です。そしてあなたの職業は何ですか？

-watashi ha nashonaru daigaku no seito desu. soshite anata no shokugyou ha nan desuka?

- 私の職業はめかにっくです。私は自分の自動車さーびすをいたりあに持っています。

-watashi no shokugyou ha mekanikku desu. watashi ha jibun no jidoushasa-bisu wo itaria ni motteimasu.

-あなたはいぎりすは好きですか？
-anata ha igirisu ha suki desuka?

- 私はこの国が好きです、けれどもここは寒いです。私は今沢山旅行しています。あなたは旅行がすきですか？

-watashi ha konokuni ga suki desu. keredomo koko ha samui desu. watashi ha ima takusan ryokou shiteimasu. Anata ha ryokou ga suki desuka?

- 私は旅行が好きです、しかし私は今ほんの少しの時間しかありません。

-watashi ha ryokou ga suki desu. shikashi watashi ha ima honno sukoshino jikan shika arimasen.

-あなたはあなたの家族と一緒に私のところに来

- I'm Italian by nationality. I live in Naples. Do you work or study?

- I am a student at the National University. And what is your profession?

- I am a mechanic by profession. I have my own car service in Italy.

- Do you like England?

- I like this country, but it's cold here. I now travel a lot. Do you like to travel?

- I like to travel, but now I have very little time.

- Could you come visit me with your family?

- I cannot. Now I have to study a lot.

てくれませんか？
-anata ha anata no kazoku to issho ni watashi no tokoro ni kite kuremasenka?

-いいえ、それはできません。今は沢山勉強しないといけません。
-iie, sore ha dekimasen. ima ha takusan benkyou shinai to ikemasen.

2

-あなたはいつもこの家に住んでいましたか？
-anata ha itsumo kono ie ni sunde imashitaka?

-はい、私は生まれてからずっとここで過ごしています。
-hai, watashi ha umarete kara zutto koko de sugoshite imasu.

-あなたは美しい家を持っていますね！
-anata ha utsukushii ie wo motte imasune!

-はい、私たちは最近修理しました。
-hai, watashitachi ha saikin shuuri shimashita.

-あなたは庭に沢山美しい花を持っています。
-anata ha niwa ni takusan utsukushii hana wo motte imasu.

-はい、私のままは花が好きです。
-hai, watashi no mama ha hana ga suki desu.

3

-紅茶を一緒に飲みませんか？
-koucha wo issho ni nomimasenka?

-はい、きっちんに行きましょう。
-hai, kicchin ni ikimashou .

-あなたはぶらっくてぃーを持っていますか？
-anata ha burakkuti- wo motte imasuka?

-はい、私たちはぶらっくとぐりんてぃーを持っています。
-hai, watashitachi ha burakku to gurinti- wo motteimasu.

2

- Have you always lived in this house?

- Yes, I've lived here all my life.

- You have a beautiful home!

- Yes, we recently made repairs.

- You have a lot of beautiful flowers in the garden.

- Yes, my mom likes flowers.

3

- Maybe we can drink tea?

- Yes, let's go to the kitchen.

- Do you have black tea?

- Yes, we have black

-あなたはどんな食べ物が好きですか？
-anata ha donna tabemono ga suki desuka?
-私はままが用意するさーもん料理が好きです。彼女はおいしいくっきーも作ります。
-watashi ha mama ga youisuru sa-mon ryouri ga suki desu. kanojo ha oishii kukki- mo tsukurimasu.
-そして私はとてもぴざが好きです。
-soshite watashi ha totemo piza ga suki desu.
-あなたはぴざを作れますか？
-anata ha piza wo tsukuremasuka?
-はい、作れます。私は料理が好きです。
-hai, tsukuremasu. watashi ha ryouri ga suki desu.

4

-あなたはぺっとを飼っていますか？
-anata ha petto wo katte imasuka?
-はい、私は犬を飼っています。彼の名前はじょにーです。
-hai, watashi ha inu wo katte imasu. kare no namae ha joni-desu.
-彼は何才ですか？
-kare ha nansai desuka?
-彼は6才です。
-kare ha rokusai desu.
-私もいたりあに犬を飼っています。
-watashi mo itaria ni inu wo katte imasu.

5

-あなたはどいつ語を知っていますか？
-anata ha doitsugo wo shitte imasuka?
-はい、私はお父さんとそれを学びました。あなたの家族は全員どいつ語を話しますか？

and green tea.

- What food do you like?

- I like it when my mom prepares dishes with salmon. She also makes good cookies.

- And I really like pizza.

- Can you cook pizza?

- Yes, I can. I like cooking.

4

- Do you have any pets?

- Yes, I have a dog. His name is Johnny.

- How old is he?

- He's six years old.

- I also have a dog in Italy.

5

- Do you know German?

- Yes, I have learned it with my father. Does everyone speak

-hai, watashi ha otousan to sore wo manabimashita. anata no kazoku ha zenin doitsugo wo hanashimasuka?
-はい、私たちは全員どいつ語を話します。
-hai, watashitachi ha zenin doitsugo wo hanashimasu.
-あなたは他の言語を知っていますか？
-anata ha hoka no gengo wo shitte imasuka?
-私はふらんす語を少し話します。
-watashi ha furansugo wo sukoshi hanashimasu.

6

-このてーぶるの上にある本はあなたのですか？
-konote-buru no ue ni aru hon ha anata no desuka?
-はい、この本は私のです。これらはあがさ・くりすてぃーの探偵小説です。あなたはこの作者は好きですか？
-hai, konohon ha watashi no desu. korera ha agasa・kurisuti-no tanteishousetsu desu. anata ha konosakusha ha suki desuka?
-はい、彼女は素晴らしい探偵小説を書きます。
-hai, kanojo ha subarashii tanteishousetsu wo kaki masu.
-あなたは本を読むのが好きですか？
-anata ha hon wo yomuno ga sukidesuka?
-はい、私は沢山読みます。
-hai, watashi ha takusan yomimasu.

7

-あなたには家族が多くいますか？
-anata niha kazoku ga ooku imasuka?
-はい、私には家族が沢山います。お父さん、お母さん、そして2人の兄弟と妹がいます。
-hai, watashi niha kazoku ga takusan imasu. Otousan, okaasan,

German in your family?
- Yes, we all speak German.
- Do you know another language?
- I speak a little French.

6

- Is this book on the table yours?
- Yes, this book is mine. These are detective stories by Agatha Christie. Do you like this author?
- Yes. She writes excellent detective stories.
- Do you like reading books?
- Yes. I read a lot.

7

- Do you have a big family?
- Yes, I have a big family. I have a father,

soshite futari no kyoudai to imouto ga imasu.
-あなたの 妹 は何才ですか？
-anata no imouto ha nansai desuka?
- 彼女は１才です。
-kanojo ha issai desu.
- 彼女の名前は何ですか？
-kanojo no namae ha nan desuka?
- 彼女の名前はじょーです。彼女はまだ歩き方を知りません。
-kanojo no namae ha jo- desu. kanojo ha mada arukikata wo shirimasen.
-あなたの 妹 は今どこですか？
-anata no imouto ha ima doko desuka?
- 彼女は育児室にいます。
-kanojo ha ikujishitsu ni imasu.
-あなたのお父さんの 職 業 は何ですか？
-anata no otousan no shokugyou ha nandesuka?
- 私 のぱぱの 職 業 は医者です。しかし彼はいま 働 いていません。
-watashi no papa no shokugyou ha isha desu. shikashi kare ha ima hataraite imasen.
-どうしてですか？
-doushite desuka?
- 彼は休 暇を取っています。
-kare ha kyuuka wo totte imasu.
-あなたのままはどこで 働 いていますか？
-anata no mama ha doko de hataraite imasuka?
- 私 のままは不動産代理店で 働 いています。彼女は家を売ります。
-watashi no mama ha fudousandairiten de hataraite imasu.

- mother, two brothers and a little sister.

- How old is your sister?

- She is one year old.

- What's her name?

- Her name is Joe. She still does not know how to walk.

- Where is your sister now?

- She's at the nursery.

- What is your father's profession?

- My dad is a doctor by profession. But now he is not working.

- Why?

- He's on vacation.

- Where does your mom work?

- My mother works in a real estate agency. She

kanojo ha ie wo urimasu.
- 彼女はどのくらい長くそこで働いていますか？
-kanojo ha donokurai nagaku sokode hataraite imasuka?
- 私のお母さんはそこで8年働いています。
-watashi no okaasan ha sokode hachinen hataraite imasu.
- 彼女は以前はどこで働いていましたか？
-kanojo ha izen ha dokode hataraite imashitaka?
- 彼女は郵便局で働いていました。
-kanojo ha yuubinkyoku de hataraite imashita.
-あなたのお母さんは今仕事中ですか？
-anata no okaasan ha ima shigotochuu desuka?
-いいえ、彼女は店にいます。
-iie, kanojo ha mise ni imasu.
-あなたの両親は何才ですか？
-anata no ryoushin ha nansai desuka?
- 私のままは38才です。私のぱぱは41才です。
-watashi no mama ha sanjuhassai desu. watashi no papa ha yonjuissai desu.
-この写真の中にいるのはあなたの兄弟ですか？
-konoshashin no naka ni iruno ha anata no kyoudai desuka?
-はい。
-hai.
- 彼らの名前は何ですか？
-karera no namae ha nandesuka?
-これがふぃりっぷ。彼は12才です。
-kore ga firippu. kare ha jyuunisai desu.
- 彼は勉強していますか？
-kare ha benkyou shiteimasuka?
-はい、彼は学校に行っています。

sells houses.
- How long has she been working there?
- My mother has been working there for eight years.
- Where did she work before?
- She worked at the post office.
- Is your mother at work now?
- No, she's at the store.
- How old are your parents?
- My mom is thirty-eight years old. My dad is forty-one years old.
- Are these your brothers in the photo?
- Yes.
- What are their names?
- This is Philip. He is

- はい、彼は学校に行っています。
-hai, kare ha gakkou ni itte imasu.
- 彼はよく勉強しますか？
-kare ha yoku benkyou shimasuka?
- はい、彼はよく勉強します。
-hai, kare ha yoku benkyou shimasu.
- そしてこれは誰ですか？
-soshite kore ha dare desuka?
- これは私の兄のじょんです。
-kore ha watashi no ani no jon desu.
- 彼は何才ですか？
-kare ha nansai desuka?
- 彼は20才です。
-kare ha nijussai desu.
- 彼は働いていますか？
-kare ha hataraite imasuka?
- はい、彼はぷろのさっかー選手です。
-hai, kare ha puro no sakka-senshu desu.
- 私はさっかーが好きです。彼はどのくらぶでぷれいしていますか？
-watashi ha sakka- ga suki desu. kare ha dono kurabu de purei shiteimasuka?
- 彼はろんどんくらぶでぷれいしています。
-kare ha rondonkurabu de purei shiteimasu.
- 彼に会ってもいいですか？
-kare ni attemo iidesuka?
- はい、もちろん。
-hai, mochiron.

8

- あなたは車を持っていますか？
-anata ha kuruma wo motte imasuka?
- はい、私たちは新しい車を持っています。

- twelve years old.
- Is he learning?
- Yes, he goes to school.
- Does he learn well?
- Yes, he learns well.
- And who is this?
- This is my older brother John.
- How old is he?
- He is twenty years old.
- Is he working?
- Yes, he is a professional soccer player.
- I like soccer. Which club does he play in?
- He plays in the London club.
- Can I meet him?
- Yes, of course.

8

- Do you have a car?
- Yes, we have a new

-hai, watashitachi ha atarashii kuruma wo motte imasu.

-あなたはどんな車を持っていますか？
-anata ha donna kuruma wo motte imasuka?

-私たちはBMWを持っています。
-watashitachi ha bi-emdaburyu wo motte imasu.

-あなたはそれをよく運転しますか？
-anata ha sore wo yoku unnten shimasuka?

-はい、私のお母さんがよく仕事場へ運転しています。
-hai, watashi no okaasan ga yoku shigotoba he untenshite imasu.

car.

- What car do you have?

- We have a BMW.

- Do you drive it often?

- Yes, my mother often drives it to work.

8

Audio

氷を砕く
Break the ice

"どうだかね、ってどういう意味？"と少年はお母さんに聞きました。

"疑わしいってことは真実か真実じゃないか確かじゃない時よ。でもたまに真実の時もあるの。"

後に二人がスープを食べている時、少年は座って窓を眺めていました。

"早く食べちゃいなさい"とお母さんは言いました。息子はお母さんを見ています。息子は何や

"What does 'I doubt it' mean?" a little boy asks his mom.

"It means rather no than yes. But it can mean yes in other situations," the mom explains to her son.

Later the son and the mom have some soup. The boy sits and looks at the window.

"Finish your soup, please," the mom says to him. The son looks at his mom. The mom sees that he is

ら 考え込んでいる様子です。
"どうだかね" と息子は最後に言いました。

thinking hard.

"I doubt it," he says at last.

dō da ka ne, tte dōiu imi? to shōnen wa okāsan ni kikimashita. utagawashii tte koto wa shinjitsu ka shinjitsu janai ka tashika janai toki yo. demo tamani shinjitsu no toki mo aru no.go ni ni nin ga su-pu o tabeteiru toki, shōnen wa suwatte mado o nagameteimashita. hayaku tabe chai nasai to okāsan wa iimashita. musuko wa okāsan o miteimasu. musuko wa naniyara kangaekondeiru yōsu desu. dō da ka ne to musuko wa saigo ni iimashita.

大学への道
The way to university

単語
Words

1. (垂直に)立てる [(suichokuni)tateru] - put (vertically)
2. 10、十 [juu, juu] - ten
3. 7、七 [nana, nana] - seven
4. 9、九 [kyuu, kyuu] - nine
5. 〜がかかる、値段 [〜ga kakaru, nedan] - cost
6. 〜するため [〜surutame] - in order to, so that
7. おおよそ [ooyoso] - roughly, approximately
8. すでに [sudeni] - already
9. そう遠くない [soutookunai] - not far

10. そちら(の方向) [sochira(no houkou)] - there (direction)
11. その後、そして [sonoato, soshite] - afterwards, then
12. どれ [dore] - which
13. の間 [no aida] - between
14. の間に [no aidani] - among
15. ばかげたこと、キィエルバサ、ソーセージ [bakagetakoto, kiierubasa, so-se-ji] - baloney, kielbasa, sausage
16. ゆでる、いれる [yuderu, ireru] - boil, brew
17. りんご [ringo] - apple
18. を除いて [wo nozoite] - without
19. を占める [wo shimeru] - occupy
20. を通り過ぎる、近く [wo toorisugiru, chikaku] - past, near
21. コーヒー [ko-hi-] - coffee
22. サンドイッチ [sandoicchi] - sandwich
23. シリアル [shiriaru] - flakes, cereal
24. スーパー [su-pa-] - supermarket
25. チーズ [chi-zu] - cheese
26. トイレ [toire] - bathroom
27. トロリーバス [torori-basu] - trolleybus
28. ハチミツ [hachimitsu] - honey
29. ハンドバック、バック [handobakku, bakku] - purse, bag
30. パン [pan] - bread
31. ミニバス [minibasu] - minibus
32. メトロ、地下鉄 [metoro, chikatetsu] - metro, subway
33. ユーロ [yu-ro] - Euro
34. 育つ、大きくなる [sodatsu, ookikunaru] - grow
35. 映画館 [eigakan] - cinema, movie theater
36. 遠く、長い距離の [tooku, nagaikyorino] - far (away), at a long distance
37. 開く [hiraku] - open
38. 起き上がる [okiagaru] - get up
39. 橋 [hashi] - bridge
40. 湖 [mizuumi] - lake
41. 公園 [kouen] - park
42. 砂糖 [satou] - sugar
43. 座る [suwaru] - sit down
44. 始めから [hajimekara] - from the beginning
45. 止まる [tomaru] - stop
46. 時々 [tokidoki] - sometimes
47. 時間 [jikan] - hour
48. 終わらせる [owaraseru] - do (finish)
49. 集める、収集する [atsumeru, shuushuusuru] - collect / gather together, gather
50. 出て行く [deteiku] - go out, get out
51. 小さいピース [chiisaipi-su] - a little piece
52. 少し、いくつか [sukoshi, ikutsuka] - a few, some
53. 場所 [basho] - place
54. 真ん中、〜の途中 [mannaka, 〜notochuu] - in the middle
55. 人々 [hitobito] - people
56. 切り落とす [kiriotosu] - cut off
57. 切る [kiru] - cut
58. 全て [subete] - everything

59. 全ての [subeteno] - every
60. 足す、追加する [tasu, tsuikasuru] - add
61. 注ぎ入れる [sosogiireru] - pour in
62. 注ぐ [sosogu] - pour
63. 朝 [asa] - morning
64. 朝食を食べる [choushoku wo taberu] - have breakfast
65. 鳥 [tori] - bird
66. 通す/まで [toosu/made] - through / in (time)
67. 通路、運賃 [tsuuro, unchin] - passage; fare
68. 天気 [tenki] - weather
69. 到着する [touchakusuru] - arrive, get to
70. 美術館 [bijutsukan] - museum
71. 必要 [hitsuyou] - necessary
72. 普段、いつも [fudan, itsumo] - normally, usually
73. 払う [harau] - pay
74. 分 [fun] - minute
75. 歩いて [aruite] - on foot
76. 戻る、背中 [modoru, senaka] - back
77. 立つ [tatsu] - stand
78. 良い [yoi] - good

B

私は朝7時に起きます。そしてばするーむに行きます。ばするーむの中では私は顔を洗い、そして歯を磨きます。それは5分かかります。私は時々朝にしゃわーを浴びます。そして私はきっちんに行きます。私は朝にこーひーを飲みます。水をてぃーぽっとに注ぎます。私はけとるをすとーぶにかけます。私はこーひーをひきます。私はこーひーをこっぷの中に注ぎます。私はこーひーを砂糖抜きで飲みます。そして私はぼうるを取ります。私はしりあるをぼうるに注ぎます。

I get up at seven o'clock in the morning. Then I go to the bathroom. In the bathroom, I wash my face and brush my teeth. It takes me five minutes. Sometimes in the morning I take a shower.

Then I go to the kitchen. In the morning I drink coffee. I pour the water into the teapot. I put the kettle on the stove. I brew some coffee. I pour the coffee into the cup. I drink coffee without sugar. Then I take a bowl. I pour cereal into the

私はそれに牛乳を足します。私はそれにすぷーん何杯かの砂糖、またははちみつを加えます。私はりんごを取り、それを切ってしりあるのぼうるの中に入れます。私はさんどいっちを作ることもできます。私はぱんを一切れ切って、いくつかのそーせーじとちーずをぱんの上に載せます。私はそれを作るのに20分かかります。

　私は大学に行かなければなりません。私は部屋へ行きます。私は本とのーとぶっくを集めてばっくに入れます。ばっくは椅子のそばにあります。私は外へ行きます。外の天気は良いです。私は道を歩いて下ります。大学へ行くためには、私はとろりーばす7番または9番に乗る必要があります。私はみにばす9番または10番でも行くことができます。ばす停は歩くには遠くはありません。それにはやく5分かかります。私はばす停で立ちます。沢山の人々がばす停にいます。みにばす7番が入ってきます。私はみにばすに乗ります。そして私は運賃を払います。運賃は3ゆーろです。

bowl. I add milk to it. I add several spoons of sugar or honey. I take an apple and I cut it into the bowl of cereal. I can also make a sandwich. I cut a piece of bread and put some sausage and cheese on the bread. It takes me twenty minutes.

I need to head to university. I go to my room. I gather books and notebooks into a bag. The bag is near the chair. I go outside.

The weather is good outside. I walk down the street. In order to get to university, I need trolleybus number seven or nine. I can also get there with minibus number seven or ten. It's not far to walk to the bus stop. It takes me about five minutes. I stand at the bus stop. There are a lot of people at the bus stop. Minibus number seven pulls in. I get on the minibus. Then I pay the fare. The fare is three euros.

みにばすには自由なの席があります。私は座ります。ばすが5つのばす停で止まった後、私はみにばすを降ります。私は大学に着きます。やく20分かかります。私は大学を3時に出ます。私は歩いて帰ります。私はいくつかの店を通り過ぎます。私は美術館と映画館の間を通ります。そして私は橋の上を歩きます。橋は湖の上にかかっています。私は公園を通り抜けます。私は公園の木々の間を歩きます。大きな鳥が木の上にいます。私は車の横を通り過ぎます。ねこが車の下で座っています。私はすーぱーの横を通り過ぎます。私の家はそう遠くありません。それはすーぱーの後ろに位置します。私は自分の家に着きます。私の家の近くには沢山の花があります。私はどあの前に行きます。私はどあを開けて中に入ります。

There is a free seat in the minibus. I sit down. After five stops, I get off the minibus. I come to university. It takes me about twenty minutes.

I leave university at three o'clock. I go back on foot. I walk past some shops. I walk between a museum and a theater. Then I walk over a bridge. The bridge is located above a lake. I walk through a park. I walk among the trees in the park. A large bird sits in a tree. I walk past a car. A cat sits under the car. I walk past a supermarket. My house is not far. It is located behind the supermarket. I come up to my house. Near my house there are many flowers. I go to the door. I open the door and go inside.

watashi ha asa shichiji ni okimasu. soshite basuru-mu ni ikimasu. Basuru-mu no naka deha, watashi ha ko wo arai, soshite ha wo migakimasu. sore ha gofun kakarimasu. watashi ha tokidoki asa ni shawa- wo abimasu.
soshite watashi ha kicchin ni ikimasu. watashi ha asa ni ko-hi- wo nomimasu. Mizu wo ti-potto ni sosogimasu. watashi ha ketoru wo suto-bu ni kakemasu. watashi ha ko-hi- wo

hikimasu. Watashi ha ko-hi- wo koppu no naka ni sosogimasu. Watashi ha ko-hi- wo satou nuki de nomimasu. Soshite watashi ha bouru wo torimasu. watashi ha shiriaru wo bouru ni sosogimasu. Watashi ha sore ni gyunyu wo tashimasu. watashi ha sore ni supu-n nanbaika no satou, mataha hachimitsu wo kuwaemasu. watashi ha ringo wo tori, sore wo kitte shiriaru no bouru no naka ni iremasu. watashi ha sandoicchi wo tsukuru kotomo dekimasu. watashi ha pan wo hitokire kitte, ikutsuka no so-se-ji to chi-zu wo pan no ue ni nosemasu. watashi ha sore wo tsukuru noni nijippun kakarimasu.
watashi ha daigaku ni ikanakereba narimasen. watashi ha heya he ikimasu. watashi ha hon to no-tobukku wo atsumete bakku ni iremasu. bakku ha isu no soba ni arimasu. watashi ha soto he ikimasu.
soto no tenki ha ii desu. watashi ha michi wo aruite kudarimasu. Daigaku he ikutame niha, watashi ha torori-basu nanaban mataha kyuban ni noru hitsuyou ga arimasu. watashi ha minibasu kyuban manata jyuuban demo ikukoto ga dekimasu. basutei ha arukuniha tooku ha arimasen. soreni ha yaku gofun kakarimasu. watashi ha basutei de tachimasu. takusan no hitobito ga basutei ni imasu. minibasu nanaban ga haitte kimasu. watashi ha minibasu ni norimasu. soshite watashi ha unchin wo haraimasu. Unchin ha sanyu-ro desu. minibasu niha jiyuu na no seki ga arimasu. watashi ha suwarimasu. basu ga itsutsu no basutei de tomatta ato, watashi ha minibasu wo orimasu. watashi ha daigaku ni tsukimasu. yaku nijyuppun kakarimasu.
watashi ha daigaku wo sanji ni desmasu. watashi ha aruite kaerimasu. watashi ha ikutsuka no mise wo toorisugimasu. watashi ha bijutsukan to eigakan no aida wo toorimasu. soshite watashi ha hashi no ue wo arukimasu. Hashi ha mizuumi no ue ni kaketteimasu. Watashi ha kouen wo toorinukemasu. Watashi ha kouen no kigi no aida wo arukimasu. ookina tori ga kinoue ni imasu. watashi ha kuruma no yoko wo toorisugimasu. Neko ga kuruma no shita de suwatteimasu. watashi ha su-pa- no yoko wo toorisugimasu. watashi no ie ha soutooku arimasen. sore ha su-pa- no ushironi ichishimasu. Watshi ha jibun no ie ni tsukimasu. Watshi no ie no chikaku niha takusan no hana ga arimasu. watashi ha doa no mae ni ikimasu. watashi ha doa wo akete naka ni hairimasu.

C

質問と答え	Questions and answers
-あなたは 何時に起きますか？	- What time do you get up?
- 私は朝 7時に起きます。	- I get up at seven in the morning.
-あなたは 朝歯を磨きますか？	- Do you brush your teeth in the morning?
-はい、私は毎朝歯を磨きます。	- Yes, I brush my teeth every

- あなたは朝しゃわーを浴びますか？
- 私は時々、朝しゃわーを浴びます。
- あなたは朝紅茶またはこーひーを飲みますか？
- 私は普段こーひーを飲みます。
- あなたはこーひーに砂糖を入れますか？
- いいえ、私は砂糖抜きでこーひーを飲みます。
- あなたはどのくらいの時間朝食を食べますか？
- それはやく20分かかります。
- あなたは大学に地下鉄で行きますか？
- いいえ、私は普段ばすで行きます。
- ばす停へは長い時間歩きますか？
- いいえ、ばす停は遠くありません。
- ばすの運賃はいくらですか？
- 運賃は3ゆーろかかります。
- 目的地までいくつ停留所がありますか？
- 私は5つ目のばす停で降ります。
- それは長い時間かかりますか？

- Do you take a shower in the morning?
- Sometimes, I take a shower in the morning.
- Do you drink tea or coffee in the morning?
- I usually drink coffee.
- Do you drink coffee with sugar?
- No, I drink coffee without sugar.
- For how long do you eat breakfast?
- It takes me twenty minutes.
- Do you go to university by subway?
- No, I usually get there by bus.
- Is it a long walk to the stop?
- No, the bus stop is not far.
- How much is the bus fare?
- The fare costs three euros.
- How many stops are there on your way?
- I get off the bus at the fifth stop.
- Does it take you a long time?

- 私はやく20分後に大学に到着します。
- あなたは帰りもばすで帰りますか？
- いいえ、私は歩いて帰ります。
- あなたは常に通りを歩きますか？
- 初めに、私は通りを下って店の横を通り過ぎ、そして公園の中を通り抜けます。
- あなたの家はどこですか？
- それはすーぱーの裏に位置します。
- あなたの家の近くには花が咲いていますか？
- 私の家の近くには沢山の花が咲いています。

- I arrive at the university after about twenty minutes.

- Do you go back by bus too?

- No, I go back on foot.

- Do you always walk on the streets?

- First, I walk down the street past the shops, and then walk through the park.

- Where is your house?

- It is located behind the supermarket.

- Do flowers grow near your house?

- There are many flowers near my house.

9

Audio

氷を砕く
Break the ice

お父さんと幼い息子は散歩から戻りました。
お母さんは息子が両手をあげたままでテレビを見ているのを見つけました。

"何で手を挙げているの？"とお母さんは聞きました。

"お父さんがそうしてと言ったから"と彼は言いました。

お父さんが部屋に入ってきました。

"セーターを脱がせてあげたんだけど"とお父さんは

A dad and his little son come home from a walk. The mom comes into the room and sees that the son is standing, watching TV with his hands up.

"Why are your hands up?" she asks him.

"It is because of daddy," he answers.

The dad comes into the room.

"I took the sweater off him," he explains, "Dear

せつめい　　　　　て　お　　　　そふぁ　すわ
説明しました。"手を下ろしてソファーに座って
てれび　み　　　　　　　むすこ　い
テレビを見なさい"とお父さんは息子に言った。

put your hands down and take a seat on the sofa, please."

otōsan to osanai musuko wa sanpo kara modorimashita. okāsan wa musuko ga ryōte o ageta mama de terebi o miteiru no o mitsukemashita. nani de te o ageteiru no? to okāsan wa kikimashita. otōsan ga sō shite to itta kara to kare wa iimashita. otōsan ga heya ni haittekimashita. se-ta- o nugaseteageta n da kedo to otōsan wa setsumeishimashita. te o oroshite sofuxa- ni suwatte terebi o mi nasai to otōsan wa musuko ni itta.

私は映画を観に行くのが好きです

I like going to the movies

A

単語
Words

1. 13、十三 [juusan, juusan] - thirteen
2. 15、十五 [juugo, juugo] - fifteen
3. 〜の方へ [〜no houhe] - towards
4. おいしい [oishii] - tasty
5. さよならを言う [sayonara wo iu] - say goodbye
6. さらに遠く [saranitooku] - further
7. そして、後で [soshite, atode] - then, later
8. ふっとうする [futtousuru] - boil
9. アイスクリーム [aisukuri-mu] - ice cream
10. ウェイター [ueita-] - waiter
11. ケーキ、デザート [ke-ki, deza-to] - cake, dessert
12. ゲーム [ge-mu] - game
13. コメディー [komedi-] - comedy
14. サラ [sara] - Sarah

15. スープ [su-pu] - soup
16. スタート [suta-to] - start
17. ソースパン [so-supan] - saucepan
18. チケット [chiketto] - ticket
19. ハンバーガー [hanba-ga-] - hamburger
20. バス [basu] - bus
21. フィルム [firumu] - film
22. 暗い [kurai] - dark
23. 一緒に [isshoni] - together
24. 温める [atatameru] - warm (up)
25. 何か [nanika] - something
26. 会う [au] - meet
27. 甘い [amai] - sweet
28. 岸 [kishi] - shore
29. 急いで [isoide] - quickly
30. 泣く [naku] - cry
31. 金曜日 [kinyoubi] - Friday
32. 散歩をする [sanpo wo suru] - take a walk
33. 自動車 [jidousha] - automobile
34. 手に入れる、とどく、取り出すために [teniireru, todoku, toridasutameni] - get, reach, take something out
35. 笑う [warau] - laugh
36. 川 [kawa] - river
37. 着替える [kigaeru] - get dressed
38. 昼食 [chuushoku] - lunch
39. 昼食を食べる [choushoku wo taberu] - have lunch
40. 注文する [chuumonsuru] - order
41. 電子レンジ [denshirenji] - microwave
42. 道、行き方 [michi, ikikata] - path, way
43. 道路 [douro] - road
44. 買う [kau] - buy
45. 怖い [kowai] - scary
46. 払う [harau] - pay
47. 無言で、静かに [mugonde, shizukani] - without speaking, silently
48. 面白い [omoshiroi] - funny
49. 友達 [tomodachi] - friend
50. 話し合う、議論する [hanashiau, gironsuru] - discuss
51. 話す [hanasu] - talk

B

私(わたし)は普段(ふだん)3時(じ)に家(いえ)に帰(かえ)ってきます。私(わたし)は部屋(へや)へ行(い)きます。私(わたし)はばっくを机(つくえ)に置(お)きます。私(わたし)はといれへ行きます。そして私(わたし)はばするーむへ行(い)きます。私(わたし)は手(て)と顔(かお)を洗(あら)いま

I usually come home at three o'clock. I go to my room. I put my bag on the table.

I go to the toilet. Then I go to the bathroom. I wash my

す。時々 私 はしゃわーを浴びます。そして 私 は昼食を食べに行きます。私 は昼食には普段すーぷを食べます。私 は冷蔵庫からすーぷのぽっとを取り出します。
私 はぽっとをすとーぶの上に乗せます。すーぷが熱くなったら、私 はそれをぼうるの中に注ぎ入れます。私 はすぷーんを持ってすーぷを食べます。私 はすーぷと一緒にぱんを食べます。私 はきっちんの戸棚へ向かいます。そして私 はきっちんの戸棚からないふを取り出します。私 はぱんをいくつかにすらいすします。
時々、私 はぴざを食べます。私 のままは美味しいぴざを作ります。私 はぴざを一切れすらいすします。そして私 はそれを電子れんじで温めます。
昼食の後、私 は何か甘いものを食べられます。私 はけーきを食べます。けーきはおいしいです。私 はけーきと一緒に紅茶を飲みます。私 はけとるをすとーぶに乗せます。けとるの中の水がふっとうします。私 はぶらっくてぃーを入れます。私 はこっぷに紅茶とすぷーん2杯の砂糖を入れます。私 のねこも

hands and my face. Sometimes I might take a shower. Then I go have lunch. For lunch I usually eat soup. I take a pot of soup from the refrigerator. I put the pot on the stove. When the soup is hot, I pour it into a bowl for myself. I take a spoon and eat the soup. Along with the soup, I also eat bread. I go to the kitchen cabinet. Then I take a knife from the kitchen cabinet. I cut a few slices of bread. Sometimes, I eat pizza. My mom bakes good pizza. I slice a piece of pizza. Then I heat it in the microwave. After lunch, I can eat something sweet. I eat cake. The cake is delicious. I also drink tea with the cake. I put the kettle on the stove. The kettle boils. I brew black tea for myself. I pour some tea and two teaspoons of sugar into a cup. My cat also comes for dinner. I pour him some

88

夕飯のために来ます。私は彼のために牛乳を注ぎます。私は昼食の後こんぴゅーたーで遊びます。こんぴゅーたーは私の部屋にあります。私は沢山のこんぴゅーたーげーむを持っています。私はこんぴゅーたーで1時間遊びます。私は映画を観に行くのが好きです。私は友達と毎週金曜日に映画を観に行きます。私たちは今日も行きます。映画は2時間後に始まります。私はばするーむに行きしゃわーを浴びます。そして私は部屋に行きます。私は着替えて映画を観に行きます。私は家を出ます。赤い車が家の近くにあります。これは私のままの車です。私は通りを歩いて下ります。私はすーぱーを通り過ぎます。私はばす停に着きます。私はばす停で待ちます。映画館に行くには、私はばす13番に乗る必要があります。私はばすを5分待ちます。ばす13番が入ってきます。私はばすに乗り込みます。私は運賃を払います。

milk. I go to play on the computer after lunch. The computer is in my room. I have a lot of computer games. I play on the computer for an hour.

I like going to the movies. I go with my friends to the movies every Friday. Today we will go as well. The movie begins in two hours. I go to the bathroom to take a shower. Then I go to my room. I get dressed and go to the movies. I leave the house. There is a red car standing near our house. This is my mom's car. I walk down the street. I pass by the supermarket. I come up to the bus stop. I wait at the bus stop. To get to the theater, I need bus number thirteen. I wait for the bus for five minutes. Bus number thirteen pulls in. I get in the bus. I pay the fare. The bus has a lot of empty

ばすには沢山空席があります。私は窓のそばに座ります。ばすが３つのばす停で止まった後、私はばすを降ります。やく15分かかります。私は公園を歩いて通り抜けます。映画館に着くまでに10分かかります。行く途中、私は友達のとむとさらに会います。私たちは映画館の中へ入ります。

私は面白いこめでぃーのちけっとを買います。私たちはほーるに入り、私たちの席に座ります。ほーるには沢山の人がいます。

私たちはずっと笑います。

映画の後、とむ、さらそして私はかふぇへ行きます。私たちは道路を渡ります。犬を連れた男性が私たちの方へ向かってきます。

犬は大きくて怖いです。私たちは急いで通り過ぎます。そして私たちは美術館を通り過ぎます。そして私たちは橋を渡ります。橋は川の上にかかっています。私たちは川のそばのかふぇを見ます。かふぇには人があまりいません。うぇいたーが近づいてきます。さらはあいすくりーむを注文します。

seats. I sit by the window. After three stops, I get off the bus. It takes me about fifteen minutes. I walk through the park. It takes ten minutes to get to the theater. Along the way, I meet my friends Tom and Sarah.

We go inside the cinema. I buy tickets for a very funny comedy. We go into the hall and sit down in our seats. In the hall, there are a lot of people. We laugh the whole time. After the movie, Tom, Sarah and I and go to a cafe. We cross the road. A man with a dog comes towards us. The dog is big and scary. We pass quickly. Then we pass by a museum. Then we go over the bridge. The bridge is over the river. We see the cafe by the river. The cafe doesn't have many people. A waiter approaches us. Sarah orders ice cream.

とむと私はそれぞれはんばーがーを注文します。私たちは映画について話し、そして笑います。外はすでに暗いです。私たちはかふぇを出ます。私たちは家へ帰ります。私たちはさよならを言います。さらととむは近くに住んでいます。彼らは歩いて帰ります。私はばす停へ歩きます。

Tom and I each order a hamburger. We discuss the movie and laugh. It's already dark outside. We leave the cafe. We're going to go home. We say goodbye. Sarah and Tom live nearby. They go home on foot. I walk to the bus stop.

watashi ha fudan sanji ni ie ni kaette kimasu. watashi ha heya he ikimasu. watashi ha bakku wo tsukue ni okimasu.
watashi ha toire he ikimasu. soshite watashi ha basuru-mu he ikimasu. watashi ha te to kao wo araimasu. tokidoki watashi ha shwa- wo abimasu. soshite watashi ha chushoku wo tabeni ikimasu. watashi ha chushoku niha fudan su-pu wo tabemasu. watashi ha reizouko kara su-pu no potto wo toridashi masu. watashi ha potto wo suto-bu no ue ni nosemasu. su-pu ga atsuku nattara, watashi ha sore wo bouru no naka ni sosogi iremasu. watashi ha supu-n wo motte su-pu wo tabemasu. watashi ha su-pu to issho ni pan wo tabemasu. watashi ha kicchin no todana he mukaimasu. Soshite watashi ha kicchin no todana kara naifu wo toridashimasu. watashi ha pan wo ikutsuka ni suraisu shimasu. tokidoki, watashi ha piza wo tabemasu. watashi no mama ha oishii piza wo tsukurimasu. watashi ha piza wo hitokire suraisu shimasu. soshite watashi ha sore wo denshirenji de atatamemasu. chushoku no ato, watashi ha nanika amaimono wo taberaremasu. watashi ha ke-ki wo tabemasu. ke-ki ha oishiidesu. watashi ha ke-ki to issho ni koucha wo nomimasu. watashi ha ketoru wo suto-bu ni nosemasu. ketoru no mizu ga futtou shimasu. watashi ha burakkuti- wo iremasu. watashi ha koppu ni koucha to supu-n nihai no satou wo iremasu. watashi no neko mo yuuhan no tameni kimasu. watashi ha kare no tame ni gyunyu wo sosogimasu. watashi ha chushoku no ato konpyu-ta- de asobimasu. konpyu-ta- ha watashi no heya ni arimasu. watashi ha takusan no konpyu-ta-ge-mu wo motteimasu. watashi ha konpyu-ta- de ichijikan asobimasu.
watashi ha eiga wo mini ikuno ga sukidesu. watashi ha tomodachi to maishu kinyoubi ni eiga wo mini ikimasu. watashitachi ha kyoumo ikimasu. eiga ha nijikan go ni hajimarimasu. watashi ha basuru-mu ni iki shawa- wo abimasu. soshite watashi ha heya ni ikimasu. watashi ha kigaete eiga wo mini ikimasu. watashi ha ie wo demasu. akai kuruma ga ie no chikaku ni arimasu. koreha watashi no mama no kuruma desu. watashi ha toori wo aruite kudarimasu. Watashi ha su-pa- no wo toori sugimasu. watashi ha basutei ni tukimasu. watashi ha basutei de machimasu. eigakan ni ikuniha, watashi ha basu jyusanban ni noru hitsuyou ga arisu. watashi ha basu wo gofun

machimasu. basu jyusanban ga haitte kimasu. watashi ha basu ni norikomimasu. watashi ha unchin wo haraimasu. basu niha takusan kuuseki ga arimasu. watashi ha mado no sobani suwarimasu. basu ga mittsu no basutei de tomatta ato, watashi ha basu wo orimasu. yaku jyugofun kakarimasu. watashi ha kouen wo aruite toorinukemasu. eigakan ni tsukumadeni jyuppun kakarimasu. iku tochu, watashi ha tomodachi no tomu to sara ni aimasu.

watashitachi ha eigakan no naka he hairimasu. watashi ha omoshiroi komedi- no chiketto wo kaimasu. watashitachi ha ho-ru ni hairi, watashitachi no seki ni suwarimasu. ho-ru niha takusan no hito ga imasu. watashitachi ha zutto waraimasu. eiga no ato, tomu, sara, soshite watashi ha kafe he ikimasu. watashitachi ha douro wo watarimasu. inu wo tsureta dansei ga watashitachi no hou he mukatte kimasu. inu ha ookikute kowaidesu. watashitachi ha isoide toorisugimasu. soshite watashitachi ha bijyutsukan wo toorisugimasu. soshite watashitachi ha hashi wo watarimasu. hashi ha kawa no ue ni kakatte imasu. watashitachi ha kawa no soba no kafe wo mimasu. kafe niha hito ga amari imasen. ueita- ga chikazuite kimasu. sara ha aisukuri-mu wo chuumon shimasu. tomu to watashi ha sorezore hanba-ga- wo chuumon shimasu. watashitachi ha eiga ni tsuite hanashi, soshite waraimasu. soto ha sudeni kuraidesu. watashitachi ha kafe wo demasu. watashitachi ha ie he kaerimasu. watashitachi ha sayonara wo iimasu. sara to tomu ha chikaku ni sundeimasu. karera ha aruite kaerimasu. watashi ha basutei he arukimasu.

C

質問と答え

-あなたは何時に大学から帰ってきますか？

-私は3時に帰ってきます。

-あなたは家に帰って来るとしゃわーを浴びますか？

-私は時々しゃわーを浴びます。

-それからあなたは何をしますか？

-それから私は昼食を食べます。

-あなたは昼食に何を食べますか？

Questions and answers

- What time do you come from university?

- I come at three o'clock.

- Do you take a shower when you come?

- I take a shower sometimes.

- What do you do then?

- Then I have lunch.

- What do you eat for lunch?

- 私は普段すーぷまたはぴざを食べます。
- あなたは自分で食べ物を作りますか？
- いいえ、お母さんが私のために用意してくれます。
- あなたは昼食の後に紅茶を飲みますか？
- はい、私はけーきと一緒に紅茶を飲みます。
- あなたは何の種類の紅茶を飲みますか？
- 私はぶらっくてぃーを入れます。
- どれくらいの砂糖を紅茶に入れますか？
- 私はてぃーすぷーん2杯の砂糖を入れます。
- あなたはそれから何をしますか？
- それから私はこんぴゅーたーで遊びます。
- あなたは映画を観に行くのは好きですか？
- はい、私は映画を観に行くのがとても好きです。
- あなたは一人で映画を観に行きますか？
- いいえ、私は友達と行きます。
- あなたはよく映画館に行きますか？

- I usually eat soup or pizza.
- Do you make the food yourself?
- No, my mother prepares it for me.
- Do you drink tea after lunch?
- Yes, I drink tea with cake.
- What kind of tea do you drink?
- I brew black tea for myself.
- How much sugar do you put in the tea?
- I put in two teaspoons of sugar.
- What do you do then?
- Then I play on the computer.
- Do you like going to the movies?
- Yes, I love going to the movies.
- Do you go to the movies alone?
- No, I go with my friends.
- Do you go to the movies often?

- 私は毎週金曜日に映画館に行きます。
- あなたはどのばすに乗って映画館に行きますか？
- 私はばす13番に乗って映画館へ行きます。
- いくつのばす停を過ぎたらばすを降りますか？
- 私は3つのばす停を過ぎた後ばすを降ります。
- あなたはどれくらいの時間ばすに乗っていますか？
- それはやく15分かかります。
- あなたはどれくらいの時間をかけて公園を通り抜けますか？
- 私は10分かけて公園を通り抜けて映画館に行きます。
- あなたは道中に誰と会いますか？
- 道中、私は友達のとむとさらと会います。
- 誰がちけっとを買いますか？
- 私がちけっとを買います。
- あなたは面白いこめでぃーのちけっとを買いま

- I go to the movies every Friday.
- What bus do you take to the cinema?
- I go to the cinema on bus number thirteen.
- After how many stops do you get off the bus?
- I get off the bus after three stops.
- How long do you ride the bus?
- It takes me about fifteen minutes.
- For how long do you go through the park to the cinema?
- I walk through the park to the theater for ten minutes.
- Whom do you meet along the way?
- On the way, I meet my friends Tom and Sarah.
- Who buys the tickets?
- I buy the tickets.
- Do you buy tickets for a

すか、それとも探偵映画のちけっとを買いますか？
- 私はとても面白いこめでぃーのちけっとを買います。
- ほーるには沢山の人はいますか？
- ほーるには沢山の人がいます。
- 映画の間、あなたは笑いますか、それとも泣きますか？
- 私たちは映画の間ずっと笑います。
- 映画の後、あなたは家へ帰りますか？
- 私は歩きまわったりまたはかふぇに行ったりします。
- あなたは誰と映画の後にかふぇに行きますか？
- 映画の後、とむ、さらそして私はかふぇに行きます。
- 誰があなたたちに向かってきますか？
- 犬を連れた男性が私たちに向かってきます。
- かふぇはどこですか？
- かふぇは川の土手に位置します。
- あなたたちは何を注文しますか？

comedy or detective movie?
- I buy tickets for a very funny comedy.
- Are there a lot of people in the hall?
- There are a lot of people in the hall.
- During the movie, do you laugh or cry?
- We laugh the whole time.
- After the movie, do you go home?
- Sometimes I walk around or I go to a cafe.
- With whom do you go to the cafe after the movie?
- After the movie, Tom, Sarah and I and go to the cafe.
- Who comes towards you?
- A man with a dog comes towards us.
- Where is the cafe?
- The cafe is located on the bank of the river.
- What do you order?

-さらはあいすくりーむを注文します。とむとわたし私はそれぞれはんばーがーを注文します。

-あなたたちは静かに食べますか、または話しながら食べますか？

-私たちは映画について話して笑います。

-かふぇの後、あなたたちは一緒に家に帰りますか？

-さらととむは歩いて帰ります。私はばす停へ歩いて行きます。

- Sarah orders ice cream. Tom and I each order a hamburger.

- Do you eat in silence or do you talk?

- We discuss the movie and laugh.

- After the cafe, do you go home together?

- Sarah and Tom go home on foot. I walk to the bus stop.

10

氷を砕く
Break the ice

電話が鳴っています。お母さんが電話に出ました。息子がかけているようです。

"ママ、窓の外を見て！"と息子は言いました。

"汚れたズボンを履いて水たまりで遊んでいる人、見える？それ、僕だよ！二回も転んだんだ！"と息子は言いました。

The phone rings. The mom answers the phone. Her son is calling.

"Mom! Look out of the window!" her son says, "Can you see somebody in dirty pants running on puddles? It is me! I fell two times already!"

denwa ga natteimasu. okāsan ga denwa ni demashita. musuko ga kaketeiru yō desu. mama, mado no soto o mite! to musuko wa iimashita. yogoreta zubon o haite mizutamari de asondeiru hito, mieru? sore, boku da yo! ni kai mo koronda n da! to musuko wa iimashita.

ジャックは弁護士になりたいです
Jack wants to be a lawyer

A

単語
Words

1. (に)似ている [(ni) niteiru] - look like
2. (何かを)取る [(nanika wo) toru] - get (something)
3. 800、八百 [happyaku, happyakua] - eight hundred
4. 〜ごろ [〜goro] - around
5. 〜へ運送する [〜he unsousuru] - transport
6. あげる、渡す [ageru, watasu] - give
7. おいしい [oishii] - tasty
8. お金 [okane] - money
9. どうして [doushite] - why
10. どこへ [dokohe] - where to
11. まもなく [mamonaku] - soon
12. アパート [apa-to] - apartment, flat
13. アルコールの [aruko-runo] - alcoholic
14. エリア、地域 [eria, chiiki] - area, site
15. キー、鍵 [ki-, kagi] - key
16. タクシー [takushi-] - taxi

17. データ、情報 [de-ta, jouhou] - data, information
18. ドライバー、運転手 [doraiba-, untenshu] - driver
19. バー [ba-] - bar
20. パスポート [pasupo-to] - passport
21. フライト、飛行 [furaito, hikou] - flight
22. ホテル [hoteru] - hotel
23. リビングルーム [ribinguru-mu] - living room
24. レストラン [resutoran] - restaurant
25. 安い [yasui] - inexpensive
26. 案内する、運転する [annaisuru, untensuru] - lead, drive
27. 一人の、一人用のスペース [hitorino, hitoriyouno supe-su] - single, with space for one person
28. 飲む [nomu] - drink
29. 運転して出て行く [untenshite deteiku] - drive out
30. 駅 [eki] - station
31. 荷車 [niguruma] - wagon, carriage
32. 荷物 [nimotsu] - baggage
33. 会計係 [kaikeigakari] - cashier, teller
34. 記念碑 [kinenhi] - memorial, monument
35. 起きる [okiru] - wake up
36. 銀行 [ginkou] - bank
37. 警察官 [keisatsukan] - policeman
38. 見せる [miseru] - show
39. 現金 [genkin] - cash
40. 郊外 [kougai] - suburb
41. 高速道路、ハイウェイ [kousokudouro, haiwei] - highway
42. 賛成する [sanseisuru] - agree
43. 持ってくる、運ぶ [mottekuru, hakobu] - bring, carry
44. 時々、いつか [tokidoki, itsuka] - sometime, some day
45. 写真を撮る [shashin wo toru] - take photos/pictures
46. 拾う、ピックアップする、持ち去る [hirou, pikkuappusuru, mochisaru] - pick up, take away
47. 渋滞 [juutai] - traffic jam
48. 出口 [deguchi] - exit
49. 情報、インフォメーション [jouhou, infome-shon] - information
50. 食料品店 [shokuryouhinten] - grocery
51. 信号 [shingou] - traffic lights
52. 寝る [neru] - sleep
53. 絶対〜しない [zettai〜shinai] - never
54. 続く [tsuzuku] - continue
55. 大きくない [ookikunai] - not big
56. 断る [kotowaru] - refuse
57. 地図、マップ [chizu, mappu] - map
58. 中央 [chuuou] - center
59. 町の広場 [machinohiroba] - city square
60. 電話する [denwasuru] - call
61. 働く人 [hatarakuhito] - worker
62. 燃やす [moyasu] - burn
63. 買う [kau] - buy
64. 半分 [hanbun] - half
65. 飛ぶ [tobu] - fly
66. 飛行機 [hikouki] - airplane
67. 飛行場 [hikoujou] - airport

68. 必要 [hitsuyou] - necessary
69. 物 [mono] - thing
70. 噴水 [funsui] - fountain

71. 聞く、尋ねる [kiku, tazuneru] - ask
72. 弁護士 [bengoshi] - lawyer
73. 話す [hanasu] - tell

B

今日私の友達のじゃっくが来ます。彼は飛行機で到着するはずです。彼は空港に朝9時に到着します。私は彼とそこで会わなければいけません。私は起きて、着替えます。そして朝食のためにきっちんに行きます。私はたくしーを呼びます。たくしーは15分で到着します。私はたくしーに乗ります。私は空港にたくしーで向かいます。空港は郊外に位置します。私は町を通り抜けています。街は渋滞しています。運転にはとても時間がかかります。そして私は町から出ます。たくしーは高速道路を走ります。空港へは1時間かかります。私の乗るたくしーは空港へ入ります。そして私はたくしーの運転手に運賃を払います。時間は8時30分です。じゃっくはふらいと815で到着します。私はいんふぉめーしょんですぐでふらいと815の出口はどこか聞き

Today my friend Jack is coming. He should arrive by plane. He will be at the airport at nine in the morning. I have to meet him there. I wake up, get dressed. Then I go to the kitchen for breakfast. I call a taxi. A taxi arrives in fifteen minutes. I get in the car. I go to the airport by taxi. The airport is located in the suburbs. I'm going through the city. There are traffic jams in the city. Driving takes a lot of time. Then I go out of the town. Taxi travels on a highway. It takes an hour to get to the airport. I drive up to the airport. Then I pay the fare to the taxi driver. It's eight thirty. Jack arrives on flight number eight hundred and

ます。私はじゃっくの飛行機を待っています。飛行機が着陸します。私はじゃっくを見つけます。
私たちは彼の荷物をぴっくあっぷします。
私たちは空港の近くでたくしーに乗ります。そして私たちはほてるに行きます。じゃっくはほてるに泊まります。じゃっくはお金を沢山持っていません。私は安くて良いほてるを知っています。それは私の家の近くにあります。
私たちはほてるへ向かいます。じゃっくはほてるに到着します。彼はほてるすたっふの所へ行きます。

じゃっくはしんぐるるーむを希望しています。ほてるの従業員がじゃっくにぱすぽーとを渡すように言います。じゃっくは自分のぱすぽーとを渡します。ですくの事務員は彼のでーたをこんぴゅーたーに入力します。じゃっくはくれじっとかーどで部屋のお金を払います。ほてるの従業員がじゃっくを部屋に案内し、そして彼に鍵を渡します。彼の部屋は小さいですが居心地が良いです。
部屋にはきっちん、ばするーむ、りびんぐるーむ、そ

fifteen. I ask at the information desk, where the exit for flight eight hundred and fifteen is. I'm waiting for Jack's plane. The plane lands. I see Jack. We pick up his luggage. We get in a taxi near the airport. Then we go to a hotel. Jack will stay at a hotel. Jack does not have a lot of money. I know a good and cheap hotel. It is close to my house. We drive up to the hotel. Jack approaches the hotel. He goes up to the hotel staff. Jack wants a single room. A hotel worker asks Jack to give his passport. Jack gives his passport. The desk clerk enters his data into a computer. Jack pays for the room by credit card. A hotel employee leads Jack to his room and gives him the keys. His room is small but cozy. It has a kitchen, bathroom, living room and bedroom.

Jack came to the city to study

してべっどるーむがあります。じゃっくは大学で勉強するために町に来ました。彼は弁護士になりたいと考えています。じゃっくは私に町を案内するように頼みます。私は賛成します。私たちは通りに出ます。外の天気は良いです。私たちはめとろ駅に行きます。じゃっくは地下鉄に乗ったことがありません。

めとろちけっとは2ゆーろかかります。そして私たちは地下鉄車両に乗り込みます。私たちは町の中央に向かいます。それは25分かかります。街の中央には巨大な広場と記念碑があります。記念碑は大きくて美しいです。沢山の人々が記念碑の周りにいます。彼らは写真を撮っています。そこには巨大な噴水もあります。沢山の人が噴水の近くに座ります。私たちはより遠くへ行きます。私はじゃっくに店を見せます。
あなたはそこで必要なものがなんでも買えます。そこには食料品店や、服屋などの店があります。そして私はじゃっくを彼の大学に案内します。私たちは

at university. He wants to be a lawyer. Jack asks me to show him the city. I agree. We go out into the street. The weather is good outside. We go to the metro station. Jack has never ridden the subway. A metro ticket costs two euros. Then we get into a subway car. We are going to the city center. The ride there takes us twenty-five minutes. In the center of the city, there is a large square and a monument. The monument is big and beautiful. There are a lot of people around the monument. They are taking photos. There is also a large fountain. A lot of people seat near the fountain. We go farther. I show Jack shops. You can buy everything you need there. There are grocery stores, clothing stores and other shops. Then I lead Jack to his university. We pass by the police station. We need to cross the street. The traffic

警察署(けいさつしょ)を通(とお)り過ぎます。私(わたし)たちは通(とお)りを渡(わた)る必要(ひつよう)があります。信号(しんごう)は赤(あか)です。私(わたし)たちは待(ま)ちます。信号(しんごう)が緑(みどり)に変(か)わります。私(わたし)たちは通(とお)りを渡(わた)ります。道中(どうちゅう)私(わたし)はじゃっくにかふぇと良(よ)い食(た)べ物(もの)が食(た)べられるれすとらんを見(み)せます。私(わたし)たちはばーの横(よこ)を過(す)ぎます。ばーの中(なか)には沢山(たくさん)のあるこーる飲料(いんりょう)があります。

light is red. We wait. The light turns green. We cross the street. Along the way I show Jack cafes and restaurants where you can eat well. We pass by a bar. There are a lot of alcoholic beverages in the bar.

kyou watashi no tomodachi no jakku ga kimasu. kare ha hikouki de touchaku suruhazudesu. kare ha kuukou ni asa kuji ni touchaku shimasu. watashi ha kare to sokode awanakereba ikemasen. watashi ha okite, kigaemasu. soshite choushoku no tameni kicchin ni ikimasu. watashi ha takushi- wo yobimasu. takushi- ha jyugofun de touchakushimasu. watashi ha takushi- ni norimasu. watashi ha kuukou ni takushi- de mukaimasu. kuukou ha kougai ni ichi shimasu. watashi ha machi wo toorinuketeimasu. machi ha juutai shiteimasu. unten niha totemo jikan ga kakarimasu. soshite watashi ha machi kara demasu. takushi- ha kousokudouro wo hashirimasu. kuukouhe ha ichijikan kakarimasu. watashi no noru takushi- ha kuukou he hairimasu. soshite watashi ha takushi- no untenshu ni unchin wo haraimasu. jikann ha hachiji sanjyuppundesu. jakku ha furaito happyakujugo de touchaku shimasu. watashi ha infome-shondesuku de furaito happyakujugo no deguchi ha dokoka kikimasu,. watashi ha jakku no hikouki wo matteimasu. hikouki ga chakuriku shimasu. watashi ha jakku wo mitsukemasu. watashitachi ha kare no nimotsu wo pikkuappu shimasu. watashitachi ha kuukou no chikaku de takushi- ni norimasu. soshite watashitachi ha hoteru ni ikimasu. jakku ha hoteru ni tomarimasu. jakku ha okane wo takusan motteimasen. watashi ha yasukute ii hoteru wo shitteimasu. soreha watashi no ie no chikaku ni arimasu. watashitachi ha hoteru he mukaimasu. jakku ha hoteru ni touchaku shimasu. kare ha hoterusutaffu no tokoro he ikimasu. jakku ha shingururu-mu wo kibou shiteimasu. hoteru no juugyouin ga jakku ni pasupo-to wo watasuyouni iimasu. jakku ha jibunno pasupo-to wo watashimasu. desuku no jimuin ha kare no de-ta wo konpyu-ta- ni nyuuryoku shimasu. jakku ha kurejittoka-do de heya no okane wo haraimasu. hoteru no juugyouin ga jakku wo heyani annnaishi, soshite kare ni kagi wo watashimasu. kare no heya ha chiisai desuga igokochi ga ii desu. heya niha kicchin, basuru-mu, ribinguru-mu, soshite beddoru-mu ga arimasu.

jakku ha daigaku de benkyou surutame ni machi ni kimashita. kare ha bengoshini naritai to kangaete imasu. jakku ha watashi ni machi wo annnai suruyouni tanomimasu. watashi ha sansei shimasu. watashitachi ha toori ni demasu. soto no tenki ha iidesu. watashitachi

ha metoroeki ni ikimasu. jakku ha chikatetsu ni nottakoto ga arimasen. metorochiketto ha niyu-ro kakarimasu. soshite watashitachi ha chikatetsusharyou ni norikomimasu. watashitachi ha machi no chuou ni mukaimasu. sore ha nijugofun kakarimasu. machi no chuou niha kyodaina hiroba to kinenhi ga arimasu. kinenhi ha ookikute utsukushii desu. takusan no hitobito ga kinenhi no mawarini imasu. karera ha shashinn wo totte imasu. sokoni ha kyodaina funsui mo arimasu. takusan no hito ga funsui no chikaku ni suwarimasu. watashitachi ha yori tooku he ikimasu. watashi ha jakku ni mise wo misemasu. anata ha sokode hitsuyounamono ga nandemo kaemasu. Soko niha shokuryouhintenya, fukuya nado no mise ga arimasu. soshite watashi ha jakku wo kare no daigaku ni annai shimasu. watashitachi ha keisatsusho wo toorisugimasu. watashitachi ha toori wo wataru hitsuyou ga arimasu. shingou ha aka desu. watashitachi ha machimasu. shingou ga midori ni kawarimasu. watashitachi ha toori wo watarimasu. douchu watashi ha jakku ni kafe to ii tabemono ga taberareru resutoran wo misemasu. watashitachi ha ba- no yoko wo sugimasu. ba- no naka niha takusan no aruko-ru inryou ga arimasu.

C

質問と答え / Questions and answers

- 今日は誰が来ますか？
- Who is coming today?

- 今日は私の友達のじゃっくが到着します。
- Today my friend Jack is arriving.

- 彼はどの乗り物で到着しますか？
- What transport is he supposed to arrive on?

- 彼は飛行機で来る予定です。
- He is supposed to come by airplane.

- 彼は何時に到着しますか？
- At what time is he arriving?

- 朝9時に彼は空港にいます。
- At nine in the morning he will be at the airport.

- あなたは彼に会う予定ですか？
- Are you going to meet him?

- はい、私は彼に会わなければなりません。
- Yes, I have to meet him.

- あなたは朝食のためにどこに行きますか？

- 私は朝食のためにきっちんに行きます。
- あなたは空港にばすで行きますか、それともたくしーを呼びますか？
- 私はたくしーを呼びます。
- どれくらい早くたくしーは来ますか？
- たくしーは15分で到着します。
- 空港はどこですか？
- 空港は郊外に位置します。
- 町は渋滞していますか？
- はい、町は渋滞しています。
- 空港へ行くのにどれくらい時間がかかりますか？
- 空港に行くには1時間かかります。
- じゃっくはどのふらいとで到着しますか？
- じゃっくはふらいと815で到着します。
- あなたはへるぷですくで何を聞きますか？
- 私はへるぷですくでふらいと815の出口はどこか聞きます。
- あなたは空港で何をしていますか？

- Where do you go for breakfast?
- I go to the kitchen for breakfast.
- Will you go to the airport by bus or will you call a taxi?
- I will call a taxi.
- How soon does the taxi arrive?
- The taxi arrives in fifteen minutes.
- Where is the airport?
- The airport is located in the suburbs.
- Are there traffic jams in the city?
- Yes, there are traffic jams in the city.
- How long does it take to get to the airport?
- It takes an hour to get to the airport.
- Which flight does Jack arrive on?
- Jack arrives on flight eight

- 私はじゃっくの飛行機を待っています。
- あなたとじゃっくはかふぇに行きますか？
- いいえ、私たちは彼の荷物をぴっくあっぷします。
- あなたたちはばす停へ行きますか？
- いいえ、私たちは空港の近くでたくしーに乗ります。
- あなたたちはどこに行きますか？
- 私たちはほてるへ行きます。
- じゃっくはほてるに泊まりますか、それともあぱーとに泊まりますか？
- じゃっくはほてるに住みます。
- じゃっくは沢山お金を持っていますか？
- いいえ、じゃっくはお金を沢山持っていません。
- あなたはじゃっくが安いほてるを探すのを手伝いますか？
- はい、私は安くて良いほてるを知っています。
- あなたはそれがどこにあるか言いますか？

- hundred and fifteen.
- What do you ask at the help desk?
- I ask at the help desk where the exit for flight eight hundred and fifteen will be.
- What are you doing at the airport?
- I'm waiting for Jack's plane.
- Do you and Jack go to a cafe?
- No, we pick up his luggage.
- Do you go to a bus stop?
- No, we get in a taxi near the airport.
- Where are you going?
- We're going to a hotel.
- Will Jack stay in a hotel or an apartment?
- Jack will live at a hotel.
- Does Jack have a lot of money?
- No, Jack does not have a lot of money.
- Will you help Jack find a

- それは 私の家の近くにあります。
- あなたたちはあなたの家へ行きますか、またはほてるへ行きますか？
- 私たちはほてるへ行きます。
- じゃっくはどこへ行きますか？
- じゃっくはほてるに入ります。
- 彼は誰に近づきますか？
- 彼はほてるの従業員に近づきます。
- どのような部屋をじゃっくは希望しますか？
- じゃっくはしんぐるるーむを希望します。
- ほてるの従業員はじゃっくに何を聞きますか？
- ほてるの従業員はじゃっくにぱすぽーとを渡すように言います。
- じゃっくは彼のぱすぽーとを渡しますか？
- はい、じゃっくは彼のぱすぽーとを渡します。
- 誰が彼のぱすぽーとの情報を入力しますか？
- ですくの事務員が彼のでーたをこんぴゅーたー

cheap hotel?

- Yes, I know a good and cheap hotel.

- Will you say where it is?

- It is near my house.

- Do you drive up to your house or the hotel?

- We drive up to the hotel.

- Where does Jack go?

- Jack enters the hotel.

- Whom does he approach?

- He approaches a hotel employee.

- What kind of room does Jack want?

- Jack wants a single room.

- What does the hotel worker ask Jack?

- The employee of the hotel asks Jack to give his passport.

- Does Jack give his passport?

- Yes, Jack gives his passport.

- Who puts his data into the computer?

に 入力 します。

- じゃっくは部屋の料金を現金で払いますか？

- いいえ、じゃっくは部屋の料金をくれじっとかーどで払います。

- じゃっくはれじ係から鍵を受け取り、そして部屋へ行きますか？

- いいえ、ほてるの従業員がじゃっくを部屋まで案内し、そして彼に鍵を渡します。

- 彼の部屋は大きいですか、それとも小さいですか？

- 彼の部屋は小さいけれども居心地が良いです。

- 彼の部屋にはきっちんはありますか？

- はい、彼の部屋にはきっちん、ばするーむ、りびんぐるーむそしてべっどるーむがあります。

- どうしてじゃっくは町に来たのですか？

- じゃっくは大学で勉強するために町に来ました。

- 彼は何になりたいですか？

- The desk clerk enters his data into a computer.

- Does Jack pay for the room in cash?

- No, Jack pays for the room by credit card.

- Does Jack receive the keys from the cashier and then go into the room?

- No, the hotel worker leads Jack to his room and gives him the keys.

- Is his room is big or small?

- His room is small but cozy.

- Is there a kitchen in his room?

- Yes, it has a kitchen, bathroom, living room and bedroom.

- Why did Jack come to the city?

- Jack came to the city to study at university.

- What does he want to become?

- 彼は弁護士になりたいです。
- じゃっくはあなたに何を頼みますか？
- じゃっくは私に町を案内するように頼みました。
- あなたは賛成しますか、それとも拒否しますか？
- 私は賛成します。
- あなたたちはどこに行きますか？
- 私たちは外に行きます。
- 外の天気はどうですか？
- 外の天気は良いです。
- あなたたちはどこへ行きますか？
- 私たちは地下鉄の駅へ行きます。
- じゃっくは地下鉄に乗ったことがありますか？
- じゃっくは地下鉄に乗ったことがありません。
- 地下鉄の運賃はいくらですか？
- 地下鉄の運賃は２ゆーろかかります。
- あなたたちはどこへ行きますか？
- 私たちは町の広場へ行きます。
- そこへ行くにはどのくらいの時間がかかります

- He wants to become a lawyer.
- What does Jack ask you for?
- Jack asks me to show him the city.
- Do you agree or refuse?
- I agree.
- Where do you go?
- We go outside.
- What's the weather like outside?
- Outside the weather is good.
- Where do you go?
- We go to the subway station.
- Has Jack ever ridden a subway?
- Jack has never ridden a subway.
- How much is the fare on the subway?
- The subway fare costs two euros.
- Where are you going?
- We're going to the city

か？
- そこへ行くには25分かかります。
- 町の中央には何がありますか？
- そこには巨大な広場、そして中心には記念碑があります。
- 記念碑はどのような感じですか？
- 記念碑は大きくて美しいです。
- 記念碑の周りには人は何人いますか？
- 記念碑の周りには沢山の人がいます。
- 彼らは何をしていますか？
- 彼らは写真を撮っています。
- 他になにがありますか？
- そこには大きな噴水もあります。
- 噴水には人が沢山いますか、それとも少ないですか？
- 沢山の人が噴水に座っています。
- あなたは他にはじゃっくに何を紹介しますか？
- 私はじゃっくに店を見せます。
- あなたは必要なものをすべてそこで買うことが

- How much time does the ride there take?
- The ride there takes us twenty-five minutes.
- What is there in the city center?
- There is a large square and a monument in the center.
- What is the monument like?
- The monument is big and beautiful.
- How many people are there around the monument?
- There are a lot of people around the monument.
- What are they doing?
- They are taking pictures.
- What else is there?
- There is also a large fountain.
- Are there many or few people at the fountain?
- A lot of people are sitting at the fountain.

できますか？
- あなたは必要なものはすべてそこで買うことができます。
- どのような店がそこにはありますか？
- 食料品店、服屋そして他にも様々な店があります。
- あなたはじゃっくをどこに案内しますか？
- 私はじゃっくを彼の大学に案内します。
- あなたたちはどのような建物を通り過ぎますか？
- 私たちは警察署を通り過ぎます。
- あなたたちは道路を渡る必要がありますか？
- はい、私たちは道路を渡る必要があります。
- どのようならいとが信号に点灯していますか？
- 信号には赤のらいとが点灯しています。
- あなたたちは赤信号で渡りますか、それとも緑の信号を待ちますか？
- 私たちは緑信号が点灯するのを待

- What else do you show Jack?
- I show Jack shops.
- Can you buy all necessary things there?
- You can buy everything you need there.
- What kind of shops are there?
- There are grocery stores, clothing stores and other shops.
- Where do you lead Jack?
- I lead Jack to his university.
- What kind of building do you go past?
- We go past a police station.
- Do you need to cross the road?
- Yes, we need to cross the road.
- What kind of light is lit at the traffic lights?
- There is a red light at the traffic lights.
- Do you walk on a red light or

っています。
- あなたは道路を渡りますか、それとも立ち続けますか？
- 私たちは道路を渡ります。
- あなたはじゃっくにどこで食事ができるかを見せますか？
- はい、道中、私はじゃっくにかふぇとれすとらんを見せます。
- あなたたちはどのような場所の横を通り過ぎますか？
- 私たちはばーの横を通り過ぎます。
- ばーにはあるこーる飲料が沢山ありますか、それとも少ないですか？
- ばーには沢山のあるこーる飲料があります。

wait for a green light?
- We are waiting for the green light to light up.
- Do you cross the road or continue to stand?
- We cross the road.
- Do you show Jack where you can eat?
- Yes, on the way, I show Jack cafes and restaurants where you can eat.
- What kind of place do you pass?
- We pass a bar.
- Are there many or few alcoholic beverages in the bar?
- There are a lot alcoholic beverages in the bar.

11

Audio

氷を砕く
Break the ice

幼(おさな)いロバートはおじいちゃんにシンデレラを読(よ)んでもらうのが好きでした。おじいちゃんはすでに本(ほん)のセリフを一言一句(いちごんいっく)知っています。ロバートはおじいちゃんにもう一回(いっかい)読(よ)んで欲(ほ)しいとお願(ねが)いしまし

Little Robert likes it when his granddad reads him the book about Cinderella. His granddad already knows every word, on every page by heart. Robert asks him to read

たが、おじいちゃんは車にメガネを忘れていたので本を読む事はできません。幸運にも彼は物語をよく知っているので、字は読めなくても読むフリをし始めました。

シンデレラの叔母が魔法をかける時のことです。

"古い車を、新品の車に変えておくれ"

とおじいちゃんは言いました。

ロバートは怪しげにおじいちゃんを見つめ、こう言ったのです。

"待って、おじいちゃん。メガネ持ってきてあげる"

Cinderella again, however his granddad's glasses are in his car. Luckily, he knows the story very well. So, the granddad takes the book and pretends to "read". He comes to the moment when Cinderella's aunt does the magic.

"The aunt turned an old Ford into a gold cart," the granddad "reads".

Little Robert looks at him attentively.

"Wait granddad," the boy says, "I will bring you your glasses."

osanai Roba-To wa ojiichan ni Shinderera o yondemorau no ga suki deshita. ojiichan wa sudeni hon no serifu o hitokoto ichi ku shitteimasu. Roba-To wa ojiichan ni mō ichi kai yonde hoshii to onegaishimashita ga, ojiichan wa kuruma ni megane o wasureteita node hon o yomu koto wa dekimasen. kōun ni mo kare wa monogatari o yoku shitteiru node, ji wa yomenakute mo yomu furi o shihajimemashita. Shinderera no oba ga mahō o kakeru toki no koto desu. furui kuruma o, shinpin no kuruma ni kaete okure to ojiichan wa iimashita. Roba-To wa ayashige ni ojiichan o mitsume, kō itta no desu. matte, ojiichan. megane mottekiteageru

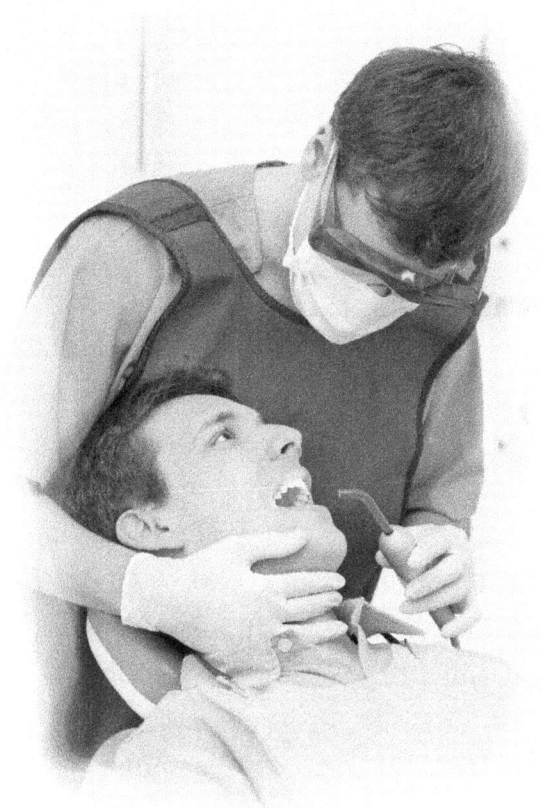

ジャックは病気です
Jack is sick

A

単語
Words

1. 19、十九 [juukyuu, juukyuu] - nineteen
2. 〜なので、だから、それによって [〜nanode, dakara, soreniyotte] - so, because of this
3. 〜になる [〜ninaru] - become
4. （数）回 [(suu)kai] - time(s) (as in "how many times")
5. ここ(方向) [koko (houkou)] - here (direction)
6. つかむ [tsukamu] - grab
7. なぜなら [nazenara] - because
8. クリニック [kurinikku] - clinic
9. コインランドリー [koinrandori-] - laundromat, launderette
10. コンサルタント [konsarutanto] - consultant
11. テクノロジー [tekunoroji-] - technology
12. デザイン [dezain] - design

13. トンネル [tonneru] - tunnel
14. ドラッグストア [doraggusutoa] - drugstore
15. ビーチ、砂浜、(川辺の)浜 [bi-chi, (kawabeno)hama] - beach
16. 一週間 [ichishuukan] - week
17. 泳ぐ [oyogu] - swim
18. 価値、価格、値段 [kachi, kakaku, nedan] - value, price
19. 感じる、調子 [kanjiru, choushi] - feel
20. 間に合う、〜が十分 [maniau, 〜ga juubun] - be enough
21. 丘、山 [oka, yama] - hill, mountain
22. 劇場 [gekijou] - theater
23. 雇用、仕事、職 [koyou, shigoto, shoku] - employment, job
24. 高い [takai] - expensive
25. 歯 [ha] - tooth
26. 歯医者 [haisha] - dentist
27. 治療 [chiryou] - treatment
28. 治療してもらう [chiryoushitemorau] - get treated
29. 図書館 [toshokan] - library
30. 生徒 [seito] - student, pupil
31. 製品、食品 [seihin, shokuhin] - products, food
32. 洗う、洗濯する [arau, sentakusuru] - wash, launder
33. 大学の生徒、大学生 [daigakuno seito, daigakusei] - university student
34. 探す [sagasu] - search, look for
35. 暖かい [atatakai] - warm
36. 地球、地面、土 [chikyuu, jimen, tsuchi] - earth, ground, soil
37. 提案 [teian] - suggestion
38. 提案する [teiansuru] - suggest, offer
39. 提出する、戻す [teishutsusuru, modosu] - give in, return
40. 動く、引っ越す [ugoku, hikkosu] - move
41. 日 [hi] - day
42. 病気である [byoukidearu] - be sick
43. 保険 [hoken] - insurance
44. 木々、草木 [kigi, kusaki] - greenery
45. 良くなる [yokunaru] - better
46. 列車 [ressha] - train

B

じゃっくは大学生です。彼は19才です。彼はてくのろじーとでざいんの大学で学んでいます。彼はばすまたは地下鉄で大学に行けます。じゃっくは普段地下鉄で行きます。
運賃は2ゆーろです。彼は地下鉄にやく20

Jack is a college student. He is nineteen. He is studying at the University of Technology and Design. He can get to the university by bus or subway. Jack usually goes by subway.

分乗ります。地下鉄電車は始めに地下を動き、そしてその後、それは川の上の橋を通ります。じゃっくは普段自分のために食べ物を用意しません。私たちの町ではれすとらんは高いため、じゃっくは普段かふぇで食事をします。

彼はまたすーぱーに行って食品を買うこともあります。じゃっくはこいんらんどりーに行き衣服を洗濯します。じゃっくの部屋に洗濯機はありません。彼はこいんらんどりーの洗濯機に汚い衣服を入れます。じゃっくはこの町が好きです。彼は常に大きな町に住みたいと考えていました。その町は美しいです。それは川の土手に位置します。その町には沢山面白いところがあります。沢山のつあー客がここに来ます。じゃっくは病気です。彼は虫歯です。彼はくりにっくに行きます。じゃっくは歯医者に行きます。彼は保険に入っているため、治療の値段の半分を払います。治療の後、じゃっくは良くなります。彼は大学へ行き、そして調子が良くなり

The fare is two euros. He rides the subway for about twenty minutes. The subway train moves underground at first, and afterwards, it goes on the bridge over the river.

Jack usually does not prepare food himself. In our city restaurants are expensive, so Jack usually eats in a cafe. He also goes to the supermarket to buy food.

Jack goes to the laundromat to wash his clothes. Jack has no washing machine in his room. He gives dirty clothes to the laundromat.

Jack likes this city. He always wanted to live in a big city. The city is beautiful. It is located on the banks of the river. The city has many places of interest. A lot of tourists come here.

Jack is sick. He has a toothache. He goes to the clinic. Jack goes to the dentist. He has insurance, so he pays half the cost of treatment. After the

ます。じゃっくはよく町を歩き周ります。彼は公園に歩きます。彼はこの町には沢山の木々があることが好きです。その町はきれいです。天気は暖かいです。じゃっくはときどき川辺の浜に行きます。彼は泳ぐのが上手です。彼は友達と映画館、美術館そして劇場にも行きます。じゃっくはこの町が好きです。じゃっくは本を読むことも好きです。

毎週彼は図書館に行きます。彼は探偵小説が好きです。彼は毎日本を読みます。じゃっくはお金を十分に持っていません。彼は仕事を探したいと考えています。彼は雇用せんたーに行きます。彼は週3回働きたいと考えています。彼はすーぱーのこんさるたんとの仕事を提案されます。彼は賛成します。

treatment, Jack gets better. He goes to university and feels good.

Jack walks around the city often. He walks to the park. He likes that there is a lot of greenery in this city. The city is clean. The weather is warm. Jack sometimes goes to the beach at the river. He swims well. He also goes to the movies, museums and theaters with his friends. Jack likes this city. Jack also likes to read. Every week he goes to the library. He likes detective stories. He reads books every day.

Jack does not have enough money. He wants to find a job. He goes to the employment center. He wants to work three times a week. He is offered a job as a supermarket consultant. Jack agrees.

jakku ha daigakusei desu. kare ha juukyuusai desu. kare ha tekunoroji- to dezain no daigaku de manande imasu. kare ha basu mataha chikatetsu de daigaku ni ikemasu. jakku ha fudan chikatetsu de ikimasu. unchin ha niyu-ro desu. kare ha chikatetsu ni yaku nijyuppun norimasu. chikatetsudensha ha hajimeni chika wo ugoki, soshite sonoato, sore ha kawa no ue no hashi wo toorimasu.
jakku ha fudan jibun no tameni tabemono wo youi shimasen. watashitachi no machi deha resutoran ha takai tame, jakku ha fudan kafe de shokuji wo shimasu. kare ha mata

su-pa- ni itte shokuhin wo kaukoto mo arimasu.
jakku ha koinrandori- ni iki ifuku wo sentaku shimasu. jakku no heya ni sentakki ha arimasen. kare ha koinrandori- no sentakki ni kitanai ifuku wo iremasu.
jakku ha kono machi ga sukidesu. kare ha tsuneni ookina machi ni sumitaito kangaete imashita. sono machi ha utsukushiidesu. soreha kawa no dote ni ichi shimasu. sobo machi niha takusan omoshiroi tokoro ga arimasu. takusan no tsua-kyaku ga kokoni kimasu.
jakku ha byouki desu. kare ha mushiba desu. kare ha kurinikku ni ikimasu. jakku ha haisha ni ikimasu. kare ha hoken ni haitteirutame, chiryou no nedan no hanbun wo haraimasu. chiryou no ato, jakku ha yoku narimasu. kare ha daigaku he iki, soshite choushi ga yoku narimasu.
jakku ha yoku machi wo aruki mawarimasu. kare ha kouen ni arukimasu. kare ha kono machi niha takusan no kigi ga arukoto ga sukidesu. sono machi ha kireidesu. tenki ha atatakai desu. jakku ha tokidoki kawabe no hama ni ikimasu. kare ha oyoguno ga jouzu desu. kare ha tomodachi to eigakan, bijutsukan soshite gekijounimo ikimasu. jakku ha konomachi ga sukidesu. jakku ha hon wo yomukoto mo sukidesu. maishu kare ha toshokan ni ikimasu. kare ha tanteishousetsu ga sukidesu. kare ha mainichi hon wo yomimasu.
jakku ha okane wo juubun ni motte imasen. kare ha shigoto wo sagashitai to kangaete imasu. kare ha koyousenta- ni ikimasu. kare ha shu sankai hatarakitai to kangaete imasu. kare ha su-pa- no konsarutanto no shigoto wo teian saremasu. kare ha sansei shimasu.

C

質問と答え / Questions and answers

- じゃっくは高校生ですかまたは大学生ですか？
- Is Jack a high school or college student?

- じゃっくは大学生です。
- Jack is a college student.

- 彼は何才ですか？
- How old is he?

- 彼は19才です。
- He is nineteen years old.

- 彼はどこで勉強していますか？
- Where does he study?

- 彼はてくのろじーとでざいんの大学で勉強しています。
- He studies at the University of Technology and Design.

- How does he get to the

- 彼（かれ）はどうやって大学（だいがく）へ行（い）きますか？
- 彼（かれ）はばすまたは地下鉄（ちかてつ）で大学（だいがく）へ行（い）くことができます。じゃっくは普段（ふだん）地下鉄（ちかてつ）で行（い）きます。
- 地下鉄（ちかてつ）での旅（たび）にかかる値段（ねだん）はいくらですか？
- 運賃（うんちん）は２ゆーろです。
- 彼（かれ）はどれくらいの時間（じかん）地下鉄（ちかてつ）に乗（の）っていますか？
- 彼（かれ）はやく20分（ふん）地下鉄（ちかてつ）に乗（の）っています。
- 地下鉄（ちかてつ）はずっと地下（ちか）とんねるを通（とお）っていますか？
- 地下鉄車両（ちかてつしゃりょう）は始（はじ）め地下（ちか）を通（とお）り、そして川（かわ）の上（うえ）の橋（はし）を通（とお）ります。
- じゃっくは食事（しょくじ）を自分（じぶん）で作（つく）りますか？
- いいえ、じゃっくは普段自分（ふだんじぶん）で食事（しょくじ）を作（つく）りません。
- じゃっくは普段（ふだん）どこで食事（しょくじ）をしますか？
- じゃっくは普段（ふだん）かふぇで食事（しょくじ）をします。
- じゃっくはどうしてれすとらんで食（た）べないのですか？

- How does he go to the university?
- He can get to the university by bus or subway. Jack usually goes by subway.
- What is the cost of travel on the subway?
- The fare is two euros.
- For how long does he ride on the subway?
- He rides the subway for about twenty minutes.
- Does the subway train ride the whole time in the tunnel underground?
- The subway train moves at first underground, then across the bridge over the river.
- Does Jack cook food for himself?
- No, Jack usually does not prepare food himself.
- Where does Jack usually eat?
- Jack usually eats in a café.

-なぜなら 私たちの町ではれすとらんは高いからです。
- 彼はすーぱーで食べものを買いますか？
-はい、彼は食べ物を買いにすーぱーにも行きます。
-じゃっくはどこで服を洗濯しますか？
-じゃっくはこいんらんどりーで服を洗濯します。
-じゃっくはこの町が好きですか？
-はい、じゃっくは常に大きな町に住みたいと考えていました。
-その町は山のそばに位置しますか、または川のそばに位置しますか？
-その町は川の土手に位置します。
- 町の中にはつあー客はいますか？
-はい、沢山のつあー客がここに来ます。
-どうしてじゃっくは病気ですか？
- 彼は虫歯です。
- 彼は薬局に行きますか、それともくりにっくに行きますか？

- Why does Jack not eat in a restaurant?
- Because in our city restaurants are expensive.
- Does he buy food at the supermarket?
- Yes, he also goes to the supermarket to buy food.
- Where does Jack wash his clothes?
- Jack washes his clothes in the laundromat.
- Does Jack like this city?
- Yes, Jack always wanted to live in a big city.
- Is the city located in the mountains or by the river?
- The city is located on the banks of the river.
- Are there tourists in the city?
- Yes, a lot of tourists come here.
- Why is Jack sick?
- He has a toothache.

- 彼はくりにっくに行きます。じゃっくは医者に行きます。

- じゃっくはどの医者に行きますか？

- じゃっくは歯医者に行きます。

- 歯医者に治療してもらうのはじゃっくにとって高いですか？

- 彼は保険に入っているため、治療の半分の値段を払います。

- じゃっくは治療の後どう感じますか？

- じゃっくは良くなります。彼は大学に行き、そして調子が良くなります。

- じゃっくは町を歩き回るのが好きですか？

- はい、じゃっくはよく町を歩き回ります。

- じゃっくはどこを歩きますか？

- 彼は公園の中を歩きます。彼は町にたくさん木々があるところが好きです。

- じゃっくは泳ぎますか？

- はい、じゃっくは上手に泳ぎます。彼は時々川の浜に行きます。

- Does he go to the pharmacy or clinic?

- He goes to the clinic. Jack goes to the doctor.

- Which doctor does Jack go to?

- Jack goes to the dentist.

- Is it expensive for Jack to be treated by the dentist?

- He has insurance, so he pays half the cost of treatment.

- How does Jack feel after the treatment?

- Jack gets better. He goes to university and feels good.

- Does Jack like to walk around the city?

- Yes, Jack walks around the city often.

- Where does Jack walk?

- He walks in the park. He likes that in this city there is a lot of greenery.

- Does Jack swim?

- Yes, Jack swims well. He sometimes goes to the beach

- じゃっくは友達とどこに行きますか？
- 彼は映画館、美術館そして劇場に行きます。

- じゃっくはどのくらいよく図書館に行きますか？
- じゃっくは毎週図書館に行きます。

- じゃっくはどのような本が好きですか？
- 彼は探偵小説が好きです。彼は毎日本を読みます。

- じゃっくは沢山お金を持っていますか？
- いいえ、じゃっくはお金を十分に持っていません。

- じゃっくはどこで仕事を探しますか？
- 彼は雇用せんたーに行きます。

- じゃっくは週何日働くことができますか？
- 彼は週3日働きたいと考えています。

- 彼はどのような仕事を提案されますか？
- 彼はすーぱーのこんさるたんとの仕事を提案されました。

at the river.

- Where does Jack go with his friends?

- He goes to the movies, museums and theaters.

- How often does Jack go to the library?

- Jack goes to the library every week.

- What kind of books does he like?

- He likes detective stories. He reads books every day.

- Does Jack have a lot of money?

- No, Jack does not have enough money.

- Where does Jack look for a job?

- He goes to the employment center.

- How many days a week can Jack work?

- He wants to work three times a week.

- What kind of job he is offered?

- He was offered a job as a supermarket consultant.

-じゃっくは提案(ていあん)を承認(しょうにん)しますか、それとも拒否(きょひ)しますか？

-じゃっくは賛成(さんせい)します。

- Does Jack accept the offer or refuse?

- Jack agrees.

12

Audio

氷を砕く
Break the ice

季節は冬です。外は雪がふっていて地面は滑りやすくなっています。お父さんは仕事から帰ってくると
「ひどい天気だ！すぐに滑ってしまう。二回も転んでしまったよ。」とお母さんに言いました。お父さんのズボンは濡れてシミがいくつか出来ていました。
ここでちょうど息子さんが学校から帰ってきました。
「外はすごく寒いよ！」息子さんは嬉しそうに言いました。「すごく滑りやすいんだ。二回も転

It is winter. It is snowy and slippery outside. The dad comes home from work.

"The weather is terrible! It is very slippery. I fell two times," he says to the mom. His pants have several wet spots. The dad is unhappy. At this moment the little son comes home from school.

"It is so cool outside!" the son cries happily. "It is

んじゃったんだよ！」息子(むすこ)さんはとても嬉(うれ)しい様子(ようす)でした。

very slippery. I fell two times!" The son is very happy.

kisetsu wa fuyu desu. soto wa yuki ga futteite jimen wa suberi yasuku natteimasu. otōsan wa shigoto kara kaettekuru to" hidoi tenki da! sugu ni subetteshimau. ni kai mo korondeshimatta yo." to okāsan ni iimashita. otōsan no zubon wa nurete shimi ga ikutsu ka dekiteimashita. koko de chōdo musuko san ga gakkō kara kaettekimashita." soto wa sugoku samui yo!" musuko san wa ureshisō ni iimashita." sugoku suberi yasui n da. ni kai mo koron jatta n da yo!" musuko san wa totemo ureshii yōsu deshita.

ジャックは新しいアパートを見つけたいです
Jack wants to find a new apartment

A

単語
Words

1. (時間を)消費する [(jikan wo) rouhisuru] - spend (time)
2. 2番 [niban] - second
3. 300、三百 [sanbyaku] - three hundred
4. 3番 [sanban] - third
5. 〜に沿って [〜ni sotte] - along
6. あれ [are] - that
7. うるさい [urusai] - noisy
8. うるさく [urusaku] - noisily
9. このように、なので [konoyouni, nanode] - like this, so
10. すぐに [suguni] - right away

11. アドレス、住所 [adoresu, juusho] - address
12. アナウンス [anaunsu] - announcement, ad
13. エージェント [e-jento] - agent
14. エレベーター [erebe-ta-] - elevator
15. オーナー [o-na-] - owner
16. キオスク [kiosuku] - kiosk
17. ノック [nokku] - knock
18. ベッド [beddo] - bed
19. ベル、リング [beru, ringu] - bell, ring
20. ラップトップ [rapputoppu] - laptop
21. 引っ越す(住所を変える) [hikkosu (juusho wo kaeru)] - move (to change address)
22. 家具 [kagu] - furniture
23. 会う [au] - meet
24. 階 [kai] - floor, storey
25. 階段 [kaidan] - staircase
26. 外 [soto] - outside
27. 革 [kawa] - leather
28. 期間 [kikan] - period
29. 拒否する、断る [kyohisuru, kotowaru] - refuse
30. 近づく [chikazuku] - approach
31. 銀行 [ginkou] - bank
32. 契約する [keiyakusuru] - enter into a contract
33. 決定、決断 [kettei, ketsudan] - decision
34. 決定する [ketteisuru] - decide
35. 月 [tsuki] - month
36. 見つける [mitsukeru] - find
37. 言う、教える [iu, oshieru] - tell
38. 考える、思う [kangaeru, omou] - think
39. 高い [takai] - high
40. 高くない [takakunai] - not tall
41. 始めに、1番 [hajimeni, ichiban] - first
42. 子供 [kodomo] - child
43. 指し示された [sashishimesareta] - indicated
44. 指し示す [sashishimesu] - indicate
45. 手配する、予約する [tehaisuru, yoyakusuru] - arrange, make an appointment
46. 宿泊施設、アパート [shukuhakushisetsu, apa-to] - accommodation, apartment
47. 招待する [shoutaisuru] - invite
48. 上に行く、昇る、上がる [ueni iku, noboru, agaru] - go up, ascend, rise
49. 新聞 [shinbunshi] - newspaper
50. 静か [shizuka] - quiet
51. 静かに [shizukani] - quietly
52. 説明する [setsumeisuru] - explain
53. 選ぶ [erabu] - choose
54. 誰か [dareka] - someone
55. 値段 [nedan] - price
56. 中 [naka] - inside
57. 中央 [chuuou] - central
58. 長い、長い間 [nagai, nagaiaida] - long, for a long time
59. 適切な、適した [tekisetsuna, tekishita] - suitable, fitting
60. 土曜日 [doyoubi] - Saturday
61. 答え [kotae] - answer
62. 同行する [doukousuru] - accompany

63. 歩道 [hodou] - sidewalk
64. 方向 [houkou] - direction
65. 本 [hon] - book
66. 明るい [akarui] - bright
67. 戻る [modoru] - return
68. 落ち着いて [ochitsuite] - calm(ly)

B

今日は土曜日です。ほてるに長い間泊まるのは高いです。じゃっくは住むあぱーとを見つけたいと考えています。彼はきおすくで新聞を買います。新聞には沢山広告があります。じゃっくはかふぇの中へ歩いて入り、そしててーぶるにつきます。彼はこーひーを注文します。彼はかふぇに座って新聞を読みます。彼はいくつか自分に適したあぱーとを新聞で見つけます。それらの値段は安いです。じゃっくはあぱーとが大学の近くにあることも望みます。彼は3つのあぱーとを選択します。彼はそれらを今日見たいと考えています。彼は広告に記載されている電話番号に電話をかけます。1つ目の番号は電話に出ません。そして彼はもうひとつの番号に電話をかけます。女性が電話に出ます。彼女の名前はしゃるろってです。彼女は

Today is Saturday. Living in a hotel for a long time is expensive. Jack wants to find an apartment to live in. He buys a newspaper at a kiosk. There are many ads in the newspaper. Jack walks into a cafe and sits down at a table. He orders some coffee. He is sitting in a cafe and looks at the newspaper. He finds a few suitable apartments in the newspaper. Their prices are low. Jack also wants the apartment to be near his university. He chooses three apartments for himself. Jack wants to see them today. He calls the phone numbers listed in the ads. The first number does not answer. Then he calls another number. A woman responds. Her name is

不動産業者です。彼は彼女と会う手配をします。じゃっくはその建物が町の中央にあるというところが好きです。彼はばすに乗り、そしてその建物へ行きます。じゃっくは到着すると、背の高い建物を見つけます。それは中央広場に位置します。そこには沢山の車と人々がいます。じゃっくはそこがとてもうるさいところが好きではありませんでした。彼は建物の外見も好きではありませんでした。それは古く見えます。じゃっくは建物に入ります。あぱーとは2階にあります。彼はどあをのっくします。女性がどあを開けます。それはしゃるろってです。彼女はあぱーとを見せるためにじゃっくを招待します。彼は中に入ります。あぱーとは広いけれども古いです。そこには大きな窓があります。それらは木製です。りびんぐるーむには大きななてれびとそふぁーがあります。じゃっくはべっどるーむに入ります。

そこには大きなべっどがあります。部屋の角にはてーぶるがあります。じゃっくはあぱーとが暗く、そして家具が少ないことが好きではありませ

Charlotte. She is a real estate agent. He arranges to meet her. Jack likes it that the house is in the center of the city. He gets on the bus and goes to the house. When Jack arrives, he sees a tall house. It is located in the central square. There are a lot of cars and people. Jack did not like the fact that it is so noisy there. He also did not like the house from the outside. It looks old. Jack enters the house. The apartment is on the second floor. He knocks on the door. A woman opens the door. It is Charlotte. She invites Jack to see the apartment. He comes in. The apartment is spacious, but old. There are large windows. They are wooden. The living room has a large TV and a sofa. Jack goes into the bedroom. It has a large bed. In the corner of the room there is a table. Jack did not like the fact that the apartment is dark and has little furniture. It looks empty. Jack tells Charlotte that

んでした。部屋は空に見えます。じゃっくはしゃるろってに今日他のあぱーとを見て決定したいと言います。しゃるろってはじゃっくに夜に電話し、そして彼の決定を伝えて欲しいと言います。じゃっくは建物を後にします。
　彼はもう1つの番号に電話します。
　男性が近くのあぱーとを貸しています。
　男性の名前はまいくです。彼は建物への行き方を説明します。じゃっくはこの場所を知っています。彼は地下鉄の駅に行きます。このあぱーとは公園の近くに位置します。じゃっくは地下鉄車両に乗ります。
　彼は地下鉄にやく10分乗ります。彼は地下鉄から降りて、道路のそばの歩道を歩きます。彼は建物を見つけられませんが、その住所を知っています。彼は子供を連れた女性に向かいます。
　彼は彼女にどうやってその建物へ行くかを聞きます。女性はこの建物を知っています。彼女はそこに住んでいます。彼女はじゃっくに行く方向を指さします。その建物は銀行の近くに位置します。じゃっ

wants to see another apartment today and decide. Charlotte asks Jack to call in the evening and announce his decision. Jack leaves the house. He calls one more number. A man rents out an apartment nearby. The man's name is Mike. He explains how to get to the house. Jack knows this place. He goes to the subway station. This apartment is located near a park. Jack goes into a subway car. He rides the subway for about ten minutes. He gets out of the subway and walks on the sidewalk along the road. He cannot find the house, but he has the address. He goes to a woman with a child. He asks her how to get to the house. The woman knows this house. She lives there. She points out to Jack the direction in which to go. The house is located near the bank. Jack comes to the house. He really likes that the house is located next to the park. It is quiet and

くは建物に着きます。彼はその建物が公園の近くに位置するところが好きです。建物の周りは静かで平和です。建物の近くには、庭があります。そこには沢山の花があります。まいくのあぱーとは3階にあります。

じゃっくはえれべーたーの中に入ります。彼は3階に行きます。じゃっくはえれべーたーから出てきます。彼はべるを鳴らします。男性がどあを開けます。これがまいくです。彼はじゃっくに同行して中に入ります。中は明るくて心地がよいです。あぱーとには新しい家具があります。部屋には大きなすくりーんのてれびがあります。それは新しいです。部屋の角にはべっどがあります。

じゃっくは部屋の中の本棚を見ます。本棚の中には沢山の本があります。部屋の真ん中にはてーぶるがあります。てーぶるの隣には大きなあーむちぇあがあります。それは革でできています。じゃっくは彼のらっぷとっぷをそこに置くことを考えます。彼はこのあぱーとが好きです。彼はまいくにこのあぱー

peaceful around the house. Near the house, there is a garden. There are many flowers there. Mike's apartment is on the third floor. Jack goes into the elevator. He goes to the third floor. Jack comes out of the elevator. He rings the bell. A man opens the door. This is Mike. He accompanies Jack inside.

It is bright and comfortable inside. There is new furniture in the apartment. The room has a large-screen TV. It is new. In the corner of the room, there is a bed. Jack sees a bookshelf in the room. There are a lot of books in the bookshelf. In the middle of the room, there is a table. There is a big armchair next to the table. It's made of leather. Jack thinks about putting his laptop there. He likes the house. He tells Mike that he wants to live in this house. He will pay Mike three hundred euros per month.

とに住みたいと伝えます。彼はまいくに月300ゆーろ払います。彼らは契約します。じゃっくは2か月分払わなければなりません。彼は同じ日にほてるから彼の持ち物をすべて運びます。

They enter into a contract. Jack has to pay for two months straight. He carries all his belongings out of the hotel on the same day.

kyou ha doyoubi desu. hoteru ni nagai aida tomaru noha takai desu. jakku ha sumu apa-to wo mitsuketai to kangaete imasu. kare ha kiosuku de shinbun wo kaimasu. Shinbun niha takusan koukoku ga arimasu. jakku ha kafe no naka he aruite hairi, soshite te-buru ni

tsukimasu. kare ha ko-hi- wo chumon shimasu. kare ha cafe ni suwatte shinbun wo yomimasu. kare ha ikutsuka jibunni tekishita apa-to wo shinbun de mitsukemasu. sorera no nedan ha yasui desu. jakku ha apa-to ga daigaku no chikakuni arukoto mo nozomimasu. kare ha mittsu no apa-to wo sentaku shimasu. kare ha sorera wo kyou mitai to kangaete imasu. kare ha koukokuni kisai sareteiru denwabangou ni denwa wo kakemasu. hitotsume no bangou ha denwa ni demasen. soshite kare ha mouhitotsu no bangou ni denwa wo kakemasu. josei ga denwa ni demasu. kanojo no namae ha sharurotte desu. kanojo ha fudousangyousha desu. kare ha knojo to au tehai wo shimasu. jakku ha sono tatemono ga machi no chuou ni arutoiu tokoro ga sukidesu. kare ha basu ni nori, soshite sono tatemono he ikimasu. jakku ha touchaku suruto, senotakai tatemono wo mitsukemasu. sore ha chuou hiroba ni ichi shimasu. soko niha takusan no kuruma to hitobito ga imasu. jakku ha soko ga totemo urusai tokoro ga sukideha arimasen deshita. kare ha tatemono no gaiken mo sukideha arimasen deshita. soreha furuku miemasu. jakku ha tatemono ni hairimasu. apa-to ha nikai ni arimasu. kare ha doa wo nokku shimasu. josei ga doa wo akemasu. sore ha sharurottedesu. kanojo ha apa-to wo miserutameni jakku wo shoutai shimasu. kare ha naka ni hairimasu. apa-to ha hiroi keredomo furuidesu. soko niha ookina mado ga arimasu. sorera ha mokuseidesu. ribinguru-mu niha ookina terebi to sofa ga arimasu. jakku ha beddoru-mu ni hairimasu.soko niha ookina beddo ga arimasu. heya no kado niha te-buru ga arimasu. jakku ha apa-to ga kuraku, soshite kagu ga sukunai koto ga sukideha arimasen deshita. heya ha kara ni miemasu. jakku ha sharurotte ni kyou hoka no apa-to wo mite kettei shitaito iimasu. sharurotte ha jakku ni yoru ni denwashi, soshite kare no kettei wo tsutaete hoshiito iimasu. Jakku ha tatemono wo atoni shimasu. kare ha mouhitotsu no bangou ni denwa shimasu. dansei ga chikaku no apa-to wo kashiteimasu. dansei no namae ha maiku desu. kare ha tatemono heno ikikata wo setsumeishimasu. jakku ha

konobasho wo shitteimasu. kare ha chikatetsu no eki ni ikimasu. kono apa-to ha kouen no chikaku ni ichishimasu. jakku ha chikatetsusharyou ni norimasu. kare ha chikatetsu ni yaku jyuppun norimasu. kare ha chikatetsu kara orite, douro no soba no hodou wo arukimasu. kare ha tatemono wo mitsukeraremasen ga, sono jusho wo shitte imasu. kare ha kodomo wo tsureta josei ni mukaimasu. kare ha kanojo ni douyatte sono tatemono he ikuka wo kikimasu. josei ha kono tatemono wo shitteimasu. kanojo ha soko ni sundeimasu. kanojo ha jakku ni ikuhoukou wo yubi sashimasu. sono tatemono ha ginkou no chikakuni ichishimasu. jakku ha tatemono ni tsukimasu. kare ha sono tatemono ga kouen no chikakuni ichi surutokoro ga sukidesu. tatemono no mawari ha shizukade heiwadesu. Tatemono no chikakuni ha, niwa ga arimasu. Soko niha takusan no hana ga arimasu. maiku no apa-to ha sangaini arimasu. jakku ha erebe-ta- no naka ni hairimasu. kare ha sangai ni ikimasu. jakku ha erebe-ta- kara detekimasu. kare ha beru wo narashimasu. dansei ga doa wo akemasu. kore ga maiku desu. kare ha jakku ni doukoushite nakani hairimasu.

naka ha akarukute kokochi ga yoidesu. apa-to niha atarashii kagu ga arimasu. heya niha ookina sukuri-n no terebi ga arimasu. sore ha atarashiidesu. heya no kado niha, beddo ga arimasu. jakku ha heya no naka no hondana wo mimasu. Hondana no naka niha takusan no hon ga arimasu. heya no mannaka niha, te-buru ga arimasu. te-buru no tonari niha ookina a-muchea ga arimasu. sore ha kawade dekiteimasu. jakku ha kare no rapputoppu wo sokoni okukoto wo kangaemasu. kare ha kono apa-to ga sukidesu. kare ha maiku ni kono apa-to ni sumitai to tsutaemasu. kare ha maikuni tsuki sanbyakuyu-ro haraimasu. karera ha keiyaku shimasu. jakku ha nikagetsubun harawanakereba narimasen. kare ha onajihi ni hoterukara kare no mochimono wo subete hakobimasu.

質問そして答え

- 今日は何曜日ですか？

- 今日は土曜日です。

- どうしてじゃっくは住むあぱーとを探したいのですか？

- なぜならほてるに長い間泊まるのは高いからです。

Questions and answers

- What day is it today?

- Today is Saturday.

- Why does Jack want to find an apartment to live in?

- Because living in a hotel for a long time is expensive.

- じゃっくはきおすくで何を買いますか？
- じゃっくはきおすくで項目別の広告がある新聞を買います。
- じゃっくはほてるに戻りますか、またはかふぇに行きますか？
- じゃっくは歩いてかふぇに入り、そしててーぶるにつきます。
- 彼はあいすくりーむを注文しますか、それともこーひーを注文しますか？
- 彼はこーひーを頼みます。
- じゃっくはかふぇで何をしますか？
- 彼は座って新聞を読んでいます。
- 彼は安いあぱーとの広告を見つけますか？
- はい、彼は彼に適したあぱーとの広告をいくつか見つけます。
- あぱーとはどこにある必要がありますか？
- じゃっくはあぱーとが大学の近くにあることを望みます。
- じゃっくはあぱーとを選択しますか？

- What does Jack buy at a kiosk?
- At a kiosk, Jack buys a newspaper with classified ads.
- Does Jack return to the hotel, or go to a cafe?
- Jack walks into a cafe and sits down at the table.
- Does he order an ice cream or coffee?
- He orders some coffee.
- What does Jack do in the cafe?
- He's sitting and reading the newspaper.
- Does he find ads for inexpensive apartments?
- Yes, he finds ads for a few suitable apartments in the newspaper.
- Where must the apartment be?
- Jack wants the apartment to be near his university.
- Does Jack choose an apartment?
- Yes, he chooses three

- はい、彼は３つのあぱーとを選択し、そして今日それらを見たいと考えます。
- じゃっくは誰と会うことを手配しますか？
- 不動産業者です。彼女の名前はしゃるろってです。
- どうしてじゃっくはこの建物を選択しましたか？
- じゃっくはその建物が町の中央にあるところが好きです。
- じゃっくはその建物には歩いて行きますか、あるいはばすで行きますか？
- 彼はばすに乗りその建物まで行きます。
- その建物はどこですか？
- 中央広場に位置します。
- 建物は静かですか、またはうるさい場所に位置しますか？
- そこには沢山の車と人々がいます。じゃっくはそこがとてもうるさいところが好きではありません。
- じゃっくはその建物が好きですか？

apartments and wants to see them today.

- With whom does Jack arrange to meet?

- A real estate agent. Her name is Charlotte.

- Why does Jack choose this house?

- Jack likes it that the house is in the center of the city.

- Does Jack go to the house on foot or by bus?

- He gets on the bus and rides to the house.

- Where is the house?

- It is located in the central square.

- Is the house located in a quiet or noisy place?

- There are a lot of cars and people. Jack does not like the fact that it is so noisy there.

- Did Jack like the house?

- No, he does not like the house from the outside. It looks old.

- On what floor is the

- いいえ、じゃっくはその建物の外見が好きではありません。それは古く見えます。
- あぱーとは何階にありますか？
- あぱーとは２階にあります。
- 誰がどあを開けますか？
- しゃるろってがどあを開けます。
- あぱーとは新しいですか、それとも古いですか？
- あぱーとは広いけれども古いです。
- あぱーとの中にある窓は小さいですか、または大きいですか？
- 窓は大きいです。それらは木製です。
- りびんぐるーむには何がありますか？
- りびんぐるーむには大きなてれびとそふぁーがあります。
- べっどるーむの中のべっどは大きいですか？
- はい、べっどるーむには大きなべっどがあります。
- その部屋にはてーぶるはありますか？
- てーぶるは部屋の角にあります。

apartment?
- The apartment is on the second floor.
- Who opens the door?
- Charlotte opens the door.
- Is the apartment new or old?
- The apartment is spacious, but old.
- Are the windows in the apartment small or large?
- The windows are large. They are wooden.
- What is there in the living room?
- The living room has a large TV and a sofa.
- Is the bed in the bedroom big?
- Yes, the bedroom has a large bed.
- Is there a table in the room?
- The table is in the corner of the room.
- Does Jack like the apartment?
- No, not much. The apartment is dark and there is little

-じゃっくはこのあぱーとが好きですか？
-いいえ、そんなに好きではありません。あぱーとは暗く家具が少ないです。
-じゃっくはあぱーとを拒否しますか？
-いいえ、彼はしゃるろってに今日他のあぱーとを見てそして決定したいと言います。
-じゃっくはさらにあぱーとを見ますか？
-はい、彼はもうひとつの番号に電話します。
-大家の名前は何ですか？
-彼の名前はまいくです。
-じゃっくはその建物への行き方を知っていますか？
-はい、彼はめとろ駅へ行きます。このあぱーとは公園の近くに位置します。
-じゃっくはどれくらいの時間地下鉄に乗りますか？
-彼は地下鉄にやく10分乗ります。
-彼はすぐに建物を見つけますか？
-いいえ、彼は建物を見つけられませんが、

- Does Jack reject this apartment?
- No, he tells Charlotte that he wants to see another apartment today and decide.
- Does Jack look at more apartments?
- Yes, he calls one more number.
- What is the name of the landlord?
- The man is named Mike.
- Does Jack know how to get to the house?
- Yes, he goes to the metro station. This apartment is located near the park.
- How long does Jack ride the subway?
- He rides the subway for about ten minutes.
- Does he immediately find the house?
- No, he cannot find the house, but he has an address.
- Can he ask somebody?

住所を知っています。
- 彼は誰かに聞くことはできますか？
- はい、彼は子供を連れた女性へ向かいます。
- じゃっくは彼女に何を聞きいますか？
- 彼は彼女にその建物への行き方を聞きます。
- 女性はこの建物を知っていますか？
- はい、彼女はそこに住んでいます。彼女はじゃっくに行く方向を指さします。
- 建物はどこですか？
- その建物は銀行の裏に位置します。
- じゃっくはその建物が好きですか？
- はい、彼はその建物が公園の隣に位置しているところが好きです。
- その建物は静かなところに位置していますか？
- はい、その建物の周りは静かで平和です。
- まいくのあぱーとは何階にありますか？
- まいくのあぱーとは3階にあります。

- Yes, he goes by a woman with a child.
- What does Jack ask her?
- He asks her how to get to the house.
- Does the woman know this house?
- Yes, she lives there. She points to Jack the direction in which to go.
- Where is the house?
- The house is located behind the bank.
- Does Jack like the house?
- Yes, he likes that the house is located next to the park.
- Is the house located in a quiet place?
- Yes, it is quiet and peaceful around the house.
- On what floor is Mike's apartment?
- Mike's apartment is on the third floor.
- Does Jack go up the stairs?
- No, Jack gets in the elevator.

-じゃっくは階段を上りますか？

-いいえ、じゃっくはえれべーたーに乗ります。彼は3階へ行きます。

-じゃっくはどあをのっくしますか、またはべるを鳴らしますか？

-彼はべるを鳴らします。

-あぱーとの中の家具は新しいですか、それとも古いですか？

-あぱーとの中の家具は新しいです。

-部屋にはてれびはありますか？

-はい、そこには大きなてれびがあります。それは新しいです。

-部屋の中のどこにべっどがありますか？

-べっどは部屋の角にあります。

-どんな家具が部屋の中にありますか？

-りびんぐるーむには大きな本棚があり、真ん中にはてーぶる、そしててーぶるの隣には大きな革の椅子があります。

-じゃっくはそのあぱーとが好きですか？

He goes to the third floor.

- Does Jack knock on the door or ring the bell?

- He rings the bell.

- Is furniture in the apartment new or old?

- The furniture in the apartment is new.

- Is there a TV in the room?

- Yes, there is a large TV. It is new.

- Where is the bed in the room?

- The bed is in the corner of the room.

- What furniture is in the room?

- There is a large bookcase in the living room, in the middle there is a table, and next to the table there is a big leather chair.

- Does Jack like the apartment?

- Yes, he says to Mike that he wants to live in this house.

- How much will Jack pay for the apartment?

-はい、彼はまいくにこの建物に住みたいと言います。

-じゃっくはあぱーとのためにいくら払いますか？
-彼はまいくに月300ゆーろ払います。

-じゃっくはまいくと最後に何をしますか？
-彼らは契約します。

-じゃっくはすぐにどれくらいの期間分払わなければなりませんか？
-じゃっくは2か月分払わなければなりません。

-いつ彼はほてるからあぱーとへ引っ越しますか？
-同じ日に彼はほてるから彼の荷物をすべて運びます。

- He will pay Mike three hundred euros per month.
- What does Jack conclude with Mike?
- They enter into a contract.
- For what period Jack must immediately pay?
- Jack has to pay for two months straight.
- When does he move from the hotel to the apartment?
- On the same day, he carries all his belongings out of the hotel.

13

Audio

氷を砕く
Break the ice

　幼(おさな)いレオンは公園(こうえん)で彼(かれ)のお父(とう)さんと一緒(いっしょ)にいます。レオンは彼(かれ)の友達(ともだち)らと遊(あそ)んでいます。

"パパ、ズボンの上(うえ)にパンツ履(は)いていい？"とレオンはお父(とう)さんに聞(き)きました。

"なぜだい？"とお父(とう)さんは聞(き)きました。

"だって、スーパーマンになれるから！"とレオンは言いました。

"わかった、じゃあ家(いえ)でやろうね"とお父(とう)さんは言いま

Little Leon is on the playground with his dad. He is playing with his friends.

"Daddy, may I put underpants over the pants?" he asks his dad.

"Why?" the dad asks the son.

"I will be Superman!"

"Okay. But let's do it at

した。
そう言うとレオンは嬉しそうに"僕はスーパーマンになれるんだ!"と友達に言いました。

"I will be a superman!" Leon cries happily to his friends.

osanai Reon wa kōen de kare no otōsan to issho ni imasu. Reon wa kare no tomodachira to asondeimasu. papa, zubon no ueni pantsu haite ii? to Reon wa otōsan ni kikimashita. naze dai? to otōsan wa kikimashita. datte, su-pa-man ni nareru kara! to Reon wa iimashita. wakatta, jā ie de yarou ne to otōsan wa iimashita. sō iu to Reon wa ureshisō ni boku wa su-pa-man ni nareru n da to tomodachi ni iimashita.

お店の中で
In the store

 A

単語
Words

1. 〜だけ、ただ [〜dake, tada] - only, just
2. いちご [ichigo] - strawberry
3. お米 [okome] - rice
4. きゅうり [kyuuri] - cucumber
5. たんす、箱 [tansu, hako] - drawer, box
6. つかむ、運転する、輸送する [tsukamu, untensuru, yusousuru] - take by, drive, transport
7. はかり [hakari] - scales
8. ぶどう [budou] - grape(s)
9. もも [momo] - peach
10. オレンジ [orenji] - orange

11. カート [ka-to] - wagon, cart
12. キャベツ [kyabetsu] - cabbage
13. サワークリーム [sawa-kuri-mu] - sour cream
14. ジュース [ju-su] - juice
15. スキャン [sukyan] - scan
16. ソーセージ [so-se-ji] - sausage
17. チキン [chikin] - chickens
18. ディスプレイ、陳列する [disupurei, chinretsusuru] - display, set out
19. トマト [tomato] - tomato
20. ニンジン [ninjin] - carrot
21. バナナ [banana] - banana
22. パイナップル [painappuru] - pineapple
23. パスタ、マカロニ [pasuta, makaroni] - pasta, macaroni
24. パッケージ [pakke-ji] - package
25. ボトル [botoru] - bottle
26. ポテトチップス [potetochippusu] - potato chips
27. ポリエチレン、プラスチック [poriechiren, purasuchikku] - polyethylene, plastic
28. マッシュルーム、きのこ [masshuru-mu, kinoko] - mushroom
29. ラック、スタンド [rakku, sutando] - rack, stand
30. リットル [rittoru] - liter
31. レシート [reshi-to] - receipt
32. レモン [remon] - lemon
33. ロールパン、コッペパン、バン [ro-rupan, koppepan, ban] - bread roll, bun

34. 違う、様々な [chigau, samazamana] - different, various
35. 一片 [ippen] - piece
36. 雨 [ame] - rain
37. 運転する、運送する [untensuru, unsousuru] - drive, transport
38. 果物 [kajitsu] - fruit
39. 会計、レジ [kaikei, reji] - checkout, cash register
40. 起きる [okiru] - get up
41. 輝く [kagayaku] - shine
42. 決定する [ketteisuru] - decide
43. 行動する、〜する [koudousuru, 〜suru] - act, work
44. 財布 [saifu] - wallet
45. 食べる [taberu] - eat
46. 成功する、無事にすむ [Seikousuru, bujinisumu] - succeed, go off well
47. 生 [nama] - raw
48. 測る [hakaru] - weigh
49. 太陽 [taiyou] - sun
50. 袋 [fukuro] - packet
51. 大通り [oodoori] - boulevard
52. 通路、セクション [tsuuro, sekushon] - aisle (in a store), section
53. 頭 [atama] - head
54. 肉 [niku] - meat
55. 日曜日 [nichiyoubi] - Sunday
56. 乳、牛乳 [nyuu, gyuunyuu] - dairy, milk
57. 入口 [iriguchi] - entry, entrance
58. 売られる [urareru] - be sold
59. 箱 [hako] - box
60. 必要 [hitsuyou] - necessary
61. 払う [harau] - pay

62. 忙しい [isogashii] - busy
63. 野菜 [yasai] - vegetable
64. 用意する、用意された [youisuru, youisareta] - ready, prepared
65. 卵 [tamago] - egg
66. 列 [retsu] - line, queue

B

今日は日曜日です。じゃっくは沢山自由時間があります。彼は店に行くことを決めます。時間は朝10時です。じゃっくはべっどから起きます。彼は歯を磨き、着替えそして朝食を食べに行きます。彼は1週間分の食べ物を買いたいと考えているため、すーぱーへ行きます。すーぱーは近くにあります。じゃっくは家を出ます。彼は大通りに沿って歩きます。外は、天気が良いです。太陽が輝いています。沢山の人々が大通りに沿って歩いています。じゃっくは歩き続けます。すーぱーはもうすぐ近くです。彼は中に入ります。じゃっくはかーとを取ります。彼は店に行き、食べ物を選びます。じゃっくは農作物の通路にいます。そこにはばなな、りんご、おれんじ、ぱいなっぷる、もも、いちごそしてぶどうがあります。じゃっくはれもんが必要です。彼はぷらすちっ

Today is Sunday. Jack has a lot of free time. He decides to go to the store. It's ten o'clock in the morning. Jack gets up from bed. He brushes his teeth, gets dressed and goes to have breakfast. He wants to buy food for a week, so he goes to the supermarket. There is a supermarket nearby. Jack leaves the house. He walks along the boulevard. Outside, the weather is good. The sun is shining. A lot of people are walking along the boulevard. Jack goes on. The supermarket is already close. He goes in. Jack takes a cart. He goes to the store and chooses food. Jack is in the produce aisle. There are bananas, apples, oranges, pineapples, peaches, strawberries and grapes. Jack

くばっくを取り、れもんを中に入れます。じゃっくはそれを3つ取ります。彼はもうひとつぷらすちっくばっくを取り、りんごを中にいれます。彼はそれを5つ取ります。彼はかーとにばっぐを入れます。じゃっくはかーとをはかりに持って行き、果物を測ります。じゃっくは進み続けます。彼は野菜売り場にいます。そこにはにんじん、とまと、まっしゅるーむ、きゅうり、きゃべつなどの野菜があります。それらは箱に入っています。じゃっくはとまととまとときゅうりを取りたいと考えます。彼は野菜を持ち、測っています。

じゃっくは肉売り場へ行きます。彼はそーせーじが一片欲しいと考えます。じゃっくはそーせーじを選びます。そこには魚、生とちょうり済みのちきん、そーせーじなどの肉製品があります。じゃっくは進み続けます。彼は卵のかーとんを取ります。肉売り場の近くで、彼は砂糖の袋を取ります。彼はぱすたの袋とお米の袋も取ります。乳製品売り場では、じゃっくは牛乳のかーとんとさわーくりーむをこっぷ一杯取ります。

needs lemons. He takes a plastic bag and puts lemons in. Jack takes three. He also takes another plastic bag and puts it in the apples. He takes five. He puts the bags in the cart. Jack brings the cart to the scales and weighs the fruit. Jack goes on. He is in the vegetable department. There are carrots, tomatoes, mushrooms, cucumbers, cabbage and other vegetables. They are in boxes. Jack wants to take some tomatoes and cucumbers. He is taking vegetables and weighing them. Then Jack goes to the meat department. He wants to take a piece of sausage. Jack chooses a sausage. There is also fish, raw and ready-chickens, sausages and other meat products. Jack goes on. He picks up a carton of eggs. Near the meat department, he takes a packet of sugar. He also takes a package of pasta and a package of rice. In the dairy

ぱん売り場では、沢山の違うぱんとぱんがあります。じゃっくはぱんを一斤と甘いばんを二つ取ります。彼はくっきーの小さい箱もひとつ取ります。じゃっくはれじに行きます。道中彼はおれんじじゅーすのぼとるを2本取ります。ぼとるには1りっとるのじゅーすが入っています。じゃっくはちっぷすも好きです。彼は2つ袋を取ります。彼は製品が入ったかーとをれじへ持って行きます。長い列がれじにできています。
じゃっくは列に立っています。じゃっくはかうんたーに食べ物を置きます。れじ係は食べ物をすきゃんします。じゃっくはくれじっとかーどで払いたいと考えています。彼はれじ係に彼のかーどを渡します。れじ係はかーどを通しますが、それは通りません。れじ係はじゃっくに現金で払うように言います。じゃっくは財布に少しだけお金が入っています。これで十分です。じゃっくはれじ係にお金を払います。れじ係は彼に領収書を渡します。じゃっくは店を出ます。

department, Jack takes a carton of milk and a cup of sour cream. In the bread department, there are a lot of different buns and bread. Jack picks up a loaf of bread and two sweet buns. He also takes one small box of cookies. Jack goes to the checkout. Along the way he picks up two bottles of orange juice. There is one liter of juice in a bottle. Jack also loves chips. He takes two packs. He carries the cart with the products to the checkout. There is a long line at the checkout. Jack stands in the queue. Jack puts food on the counter. The cashier scans the food. Jack wants to pay by credit card. He gives the cashier his card. Cashier puts the card through, but it does not work. The cashier asks Jack to pay in cash. Jack has a little money in his wallet. This is enough. Jack pays the cashier. The cashier gives him

a check. Jack leaves the store.

kyou ha nichiyoubidesu. jakku ha takusan jiyuu jikan ga arimasu. kare ha mise ni ikukoto wo kimemasu. Jikan ha asa jujidesu. jakku ha beddo kara okimasu. kare ha ha wo migaki, kigae soshite choushoku wo tabeni ikimasu. kare ha isshuukanbun no tabemono wo kaitai to kangaete irutame, su-pa- he ikimasu. su-pa- ha chikakuni arimasu. jakku ha ie wo demasu. kare ha oodori ni sotte arukimasu. soto ha, tenki ga iidesu. taiyou ga kagayaite imasu. takusan no hitobito ga oodori ni sotte aruiteimasu. jakku ha aruki tsudukemasu. su-pa- ha mou suguchikakudesu. kare ha naka ni hairimasu. jakku ha ka-to wo torimasu. kare ha mise ni iki, tabemono wo erabimasu. jakku ha nousakubutsu no tsuuro ni imasu. soko niha banana, ringo, orenji, painappuru, momo, ichigo soshite budou ga arimasu. jakku ha remon ga hitsuyou desu. kare ha purasuchikkubakku wo tori, remon wo naka ni iremasu. jakku ha sore wo mittsu torimasu. kare ha mouhitotsu purasuchikkubakku wo tori, ringo wo naka ni iremasu. kare ha sore wo itsutsu torimasu. kare ha ka-to ni bakku wo iremasu. jakku ha ka-to wo hakari ni matteiki, kudamono wo hakarimasu. jakku ha susumi tsudukemasu. kare ha yasai uriba ni imasu. soko niha ninjin, tomato, masshuru-mu, kyuri, kyabetsu nado no yasai ga arimasu. sorera ha hako ni haitteimasu. jakku ha tomato to kyuri wo toritai to kangaemasu. kare ha yasai wo mochi, hakatte imasu. jakku ha niku uriba he ikimasu. kare ha so-se-ji ga ippen hoshii to kangaemasu. jakku ha so-se-ji wo erabimasu. Soko niha sakana, nama to chourizumi no chikin, so-se-ji nado no nikuseihin ga arimasu. jakku ha susumi tsudukemasu. kare ha tamago no ka-ton wo torimasu. Niku ueiba no chikakude, kare ha satou no fukuro wo torimasu. kare ha pasuta no fukuro to okome no fukuro mo torimasu. nyuseihin uriba deha, jakku ha gyunyu no ka-ton to sawa-kuri-mu wo koppu ippai torimasu. pan uriba deha, takusan no chigau ban to pan ga arimasu. jakku ha pan wo ikkin to amai ban wo futatsu torimasu. kare ha kukki- no chiisai hako mo hitotsu torimasu. jakku ha reji ni ikimasu. douchu kare ha orenjiju-su no botoru wo nihon torimasu. botoru niha ichirittoru no ju-su ga haitteimasu. jakku ha chippusu mo sukidesu. kare ha futatsu fukuro wo torimasu. kare ha seihin ga haitta ka-to wo reji he motteikimasu. nagai retsu ga reji ni dekite imasu. jakku ha retsu ni tatteimasu. jakku ha kaunta- ni tabemono wo okimasu. rejigakari ha tabemono wo sukyan shimasu. jakku ha kurejittoka-do de haraitai to kangaete imasu. kare ha rejigakari ni kare no ka-do wo watashimasu. rejigakari ha ka-do wo tooshimasu ga, sore ha toorimasen. rejigakari ha jakku ni genkin de harauyouni iimasu. jakku ha saifu ni sukoshi dake okane ga haitte imasu. korede juubundesu. jakku ha rejigakari ni okane wo haraimasu. rejigakari ha kare ni ryoushusho wo watashimasu. jakku ha mise wo demasu.

質問と答え

きょう なにようび
- 今日は何曜日ですか？

Questions and answers

- What day is it today?

- 今日は日曜日です。
- じゃっくは今日とても忙しいですか？
- いいえ、じゃっくは沢山自由時間があります。
- じゃっくは今日どこに行きますか？
- 彼は店に行くことに決めます。
- 何時ですか？
- 朝10時です。
- じゃっくはどうしてすーぱーに行きますか？
- 彼は1週間分の食べ物を買いたいと考えています。
- 外は雨が降っていますか？
- いいえ、外は良い天気です。太陽が輝いています。
- 人々は大通りに沿って歩いていますか？
- はい、沢山の人々が大通りにそって歩いています。
- じゃっくはすーぱーの入り口で何を取りますか？
- じゃっくはかーとを取ります。

- Today is Sunday.
- Is Jack very busy today?
- No, Jack has got a lot of free time.
- Where will Jack go today?
- He decides to go to the store.
- What time is it?
- It's ten o'clock in the morning.
- Why does Jack go to the supermarket?
- He wants to buy food for the week.
- Is it raining outside?
- No, the weather is fine outside. The sun is shining.
- Are there people walking along the boulevard?
- Yes, a lot of people are walking along the boulevard.
- What does Jack take at the entrance to the supermarket?
- Jack takes a cart.
- What is sold in the fruit

- 果物売り場には何が売られていますか？
- そこにはばなな、りんご、おれんじ、ぱいなっぷる、もも、いちごそしてぶどうがあります。
- じゃっくはこの売り場では何が必要ですか？
- じゃっくはれもんが必要です。
- 彼はれもんをいくつぷらすちっくばっぐに入れますか？
- 彼は3つ入れます。
- じゃっくは他に何を取りますか？
- 彼はもう1つぷらすちっくばっぐを取り、中にりんごを入れます。
- じゃっくはいくつりんごを取りますか？
- 彼は5つ取ります。
- じゃっくはどこで果物を測りますか？
- じゃっくははかりで果物を測ります。
- 野菜売り場には何がありますか？
- そこにはにんじん、とまと、まっしゅるーむ、きゅうり、きゃべつなどの野菜があります。
- 野菜はどこですか？
- それらは箱に入っています。
- じゃっくは何の野菜が必要ですか？

- There are bananas, apples, oranges, pineapple, peaches, strawberries and grapes.

- What does Jack need in this department?

- Jack needs lemons.

- How many lemons does he put in a plastic bag?

- He puts three.

- What else does Jack take?

- He takes another plastic bag and puts apples in it.

- How many apples does Jack take?

- He takes five.

- Where does Jack weigh the fruit?

- Jack fruit weighs on the scale.

- What is there in the vegetable department?

- There are carrots, tomatoes, mushrooms, cucumbers, cabbage and other vegetables.

- じゃっくはいくつかのとまとときゅうりが必要（ひつよう）です。
- じゃっくは野菜（やさい）を取り、そしてさらに遠（とお）く行きますか？
- いいえ、彼（かれ）は野菜（やさい）を取（と）り、それらを測（はか）ります。
- じゃっくは肉（にく）のせくしょんでそーせーじをいっぺんほしいと一片欲しいと考（かんが）えていますか？
- はい、じゃっくはそーせーじを選択（せんたく）します。
- じゃっくは他（た）に何（なに）の製品（せいひん）を取（と）りますか？
- 彼（かれ）は卵（たまご）のかーとん、砂糖（さとう）の袋（ふくろ）、ぱすたの袋（ふくろ）、そしてお米（べい）の袋（ふくろ）を取（と）ります。
- じゃっくは乳製品（にゅうせいひん）を食（た）べますか？
- はい、じゃっくは乳製品売り場（にゅうせいひんうば）で牛乳（ぎゅうにゅう）のかーとん、そしてさわーくりーむのこっぷを一（ひと）つ取（と）ります。
- すーぱーには良（よ）いぱん売り場（うば）はありますか？
- はい、沢山（たくさん）の違（ちが）うぱんやばんがぱん売り場（うば）にあります。
- じゃっくはぱんだけを買（か）いますか、それとも彼（かれ）はばんも買（か）いますか？

- Where are the vegetables?
- They are in boxes.
- What vegetables does Jack need?
- Jack wants to take a few tomatoes and cucumbers.
- Does Jack take the vegetables and go further?
- No, he picks up vegetables and weighs them.
- Does Jack want to take a piece of sausage in the meat section?
- Yes, Jack chooses sausage.
- What other products does Jack take?
- He takes a carton of eggs, a packet of sugar, a packet of pasta and a pack of rice.
- Does Jack eat dairy products?
- Yes, Jack takes a carton of milk and a cup of sour cream in the dairy department.
- Is there a good bread department in the supermarket?

-じゃっくはぱんを一斤と甘いぱんを２つ取ります。
- 彼はくっきーが好きですか？
-はい、彼は小さい箱のくっきーを１つ取ります。
-じゃっくはれじへの道中で他には何を取りますか？
-れじへの道中で、彼はじゅーすを２本取ります。
- 何の種類のじゅーすをじゃっくは取りますか？
-おれんじじゅーすを取ります。
-ぼとるにはどれくらいのじゅーすが入っていますか？
-ぼとるにはじゅーすが１りっとる入っています。
-じゃっくはちっぷすが好きですか？
-はいじゃっくはちっぷすが好きです。彼は袋を２つ取ります。
-れじには列がありますか？
-はい、長い列がれじにできています。
-じゃっく列に並びたくないので食べ物を持たずに出て行きますか？

- Yes, there are a lot of different buns and bread in the bread department.
- Does Jack only buy bread or does he buy buns too?
- Jack picks up a loaf of bread and two sweet buns.
- Does he like cookies?
- Yes, he takes one small box of cookies.
- What else does Jack take on the way to the checkout?
- On the way to the checkout, he takes two bottles of juice.
- What kind of juice does Jack buy?
- Orange juice.
- How much juice is there in a bottle?
- There is one liter of juice in a bottle.
- Does Jack like chips?
- Yes, Jack loves chips. He takes two packs.
- Is there a line at the

-いいえ、じゃっくは列に並びます。
- 彼はどこに食べ物を置きますか？
-じゃっくは食べ物をかうんたーに置きます。
-じゃっくは現金で払いたいですか、それともくれじっとかーどで払いたいですか？
-じゃっくはくれじっとかーどで払いたいと考えています。彼はれじ係にかーどを渡します。
- 彼は製品をかーどで払うことができますか？
-いいえ。れじ係はかーどを通しますが、通りません。
-れじ係はじゃっくに何を聞きますか？
-れじ係はじゃっくに現金で払うように言います。
-じゃっくはお金を持っていますか？
- 彼は財布にお金を少し持っています。
- 彼は払うために十分なお金を持っていますか？
-はい、彼は十分なお金を持っています。じゃっくはれじ係にお金を払います。

checkout?

- Yes, there is a long line at the checkout.

- Does Jack not want to stand in the line and leaves without the food?

- No, Jack stands in the line.

- Where did he puts food?

- Jack puts food on the counter.

- Does Jack want to pay in cash or by credit card?

- Jack wants to pay by credit card. He gives the cashier his card.

- Does he manage to pay for products by card?

- No. The cashier puts the card through, but it does not work.

- What does the cashier ask Jack?

- The cashier asks Jack to pay in cash.

- Does Jack have money?

- He has a little money in his wallet.

- Does he have enough money to him to pay?

- Yes, he has enough money. Jack pays the cashier.

14

Audio

氷を砕く
Break the ice

"ママ、小さい時はどんなスマートフォンを使ってたの？"と幼い息子がお母さんに聞きました。

"持てなかったわよ"

"タブレット持ってた？"と彼はもう一回聞きました。

"ママが幼い頃は、スマートフォンも、タブレットもなかったのよ。"とお母さんは答えました。息子はとても驚いていました。

"ママが小さいとき、恐竜見たことあ

"Mommy, what smartphone did you have when you were little?" a little son asks his mom.

"None," his mom answers.

"Did you have a tablet?" he asks again.

"When I was little, there were neither tablets nor smartphones," the mom says to her son. Her son is very surprised.

"Mom, did you see dinosaurs, when you were a

153

る?" と息子は聞きました。
"見たことないわよ、ママはそんなに歳をとってないわ"

mama, chiisai toki wa donna Suma-To fuxon o tsukatteta no? to osanai musuko ga okāsan ni kikimashita. motenakatta wa yo taburetto motteta? to kare wa mō ichi kai kikimashita. mama ga osanai koro wa, Suma-To fuxon mo, taburetto mo nakatta no yo. to okāsan wa kotaemashita. musuko wa totemo odoroiteimashita. mama ga chiisai toki, kyōryū mita koto aru? to musuko wa kikimashita. mita koto nai wa yo, mama wa sonnani toshi o tottenai wa.

little child?" he asks again.

"No, I did not, dear. I am not that old."

私は今日クラスが４つあります
I have four classes today

A

単語
Words

1. (チェックを)書く [(chekku wo)kaku] - write out (a check)
2. (時間を)取る、持続する [(jikan wo)toru, ijisuru] - take (time), last
3. 数式 [suushiki] - formula
4. 12番目 [juunibanme] - twelfth
5. 1個半 [ikkohan] - one and a half
6. 4番 [yonban] - fourth
7. やく [yaku] - about
8. を乗せる [wo noseru] - put on
9. オフィス、事務所 [ofisu, jimusho] - office
10. サンドイッチ [sandoicchi] - sandwich

11. ステップ [suteppu] - step
12. チョーク [cho-ku] - chalk
13. テスト [tesuto] - test
14. ブリュッセル [buryusseru] - Brussels
15. ページ [pe-ji] - page
16. ペア [pea] - pair
17. ルール [ru-ru] - rule
18. 一覧、概要 [ichiran, gaiyou] - synopsis, outline
19. 鉛筆 [enpitsu] - pencil
20. 壊す [kowasu] - break
21. 海 [umi] - ocean
22. 開ける [akeru] - open
23. 開始 [kaishi] - start
24. 学長室 [gakuchoushitsu] - dean's office
25. 議題、もの、物事 [gidai, mono, monogoto] - subject, thing
26. 教科書、テキスト [kyoukasho, tekisuto] - textbook
27. 光 [hikari] - light
28. 講義室、教室 [kougishitsu, kyoushitsu] - auditorium, class-room
29. 黒板 [kokuban] - board
30. 雑誌 [zasshi] - magazine
31. 残される、残る [nokosareru, nokoru] - be left, stay
32. 司書 [shisho] - librarian
33. 始まり [hajimari] - beginning
34. 次の、次 [tsugino, tsugi] - following, next
35. 授業、クラス [jugyou, kurasu] - classes
36. 準備する [junbisuru] - prepare oneself
37. 暑い [atsui] - hot
38. 書きとめる [kakitomeru] - write down
39. 生物学 [seibutsugaku] - biology
40. 請求書、料金 [seikyuusho, ryoukin] - bill
41. 先生、インストラクター [sensei, insutorakuta-] - teacher, instructor
42. 祖父、年を取った男性 [sofu, toshi wo totta dansei] - grandfather, old man
43. 祖母、年を取った女性 [sofu, toshi wo totta josei] - grandmother, old woman
44. 地理学 [chirigaku] - geography
45. 中、中に [naka, nakani] - in, into
46. 注意深く、丁寧に [chuuibukaku, teineini] - carefully, attentively
47. 朝食 [choushoku] - breakfast
48. 定規 [jougi] - ruler
49. 届く [todoku] - reach
50. 疲れる [tsukareru] - get tired
51. 物理学 [butsurigaku] - physics
52. 平和;世界 [heiwa, sekai] - peace; world
53. 面白い、興味深い [omoshiroi, kyoumibukai] - interesting
54. 戻る [modoru] - return
55. 夜 [yoru] - evening
56. 歴史 [rekishi] - history

B

今日私は大学に行きます。私はそこに8時30分にいる必要があります。私は着替えます。外は暑いので私は薄着をします。そして私は朝食を食べます。私は朝食にさんどいっちを食べ、そして紅茶を飲みます。私は自分の物を集めます。私はのーとぶっく、ぺん、鉛筆、定規そして歴史の教科書を大学に持って行きます。私は家を出てばす停に行きます。私はばすに乗って大学に行きます。私は大学を見つけます。沢山の生徒が入り口にいます。私はどあへ行き、大学に入ります。今日私はくらすが4つあります。1番目の授業は物理学、2番目は歴史、3番目は生物学、そして4番目は英語です。私は物理学のために講義室に行く必要があります。私は2階へと階段を上ります。私は物理学の講義室へ行きます。沢山の生徒が講義室の近く

Today I'm going to university. I have to be there at eight thirty. I get dressed. It is hot outside, so I put on light clothing. Then I have breakfast. I eat a sandwich and drink tea for breakfast. I collect my things. I take with me a notebook, pen, pencil, ruler and history textbook to university. I leave the house and go to the bus stop. I get on the bus to university. I see the university. There are a lot of students at the entrance. I go to the door and enter the university. Today I have four classes. The first lesson is physics, the second one is history, the third one is biology, the fourth one is English. I need to go to the auditorium for physics. I climb the stairs to the second floor. I go to the physics auditory. A lot of students are standing near

に立っています。授業が始まるまでにあと10分残っています。私は講義室に入り、椅子に座ります。私の隣に座っているのは、私の友達のまいくです。彼はとても良い成績を取ります。私たちの先生が入ってきます。彼の名前はすてぃーぶん先生です。彼はちょーくを取り、黒板に議題を書きます。生徒たちは自分ののーとぶっくとぺんを取り出します。私たちは議題を書きとめます。すてぃーぶん先生はそれから私たちの物理学の本を配布します。彼は本の12ぺーじを開くように言います。私たちは数式とるーるをのーとぶっくに書きとめます。

すてぃーぶん先生は議題について私たちに話します。私たちはそれを注意深く聴きます。授業は1時間半続きます。そして私は講義室を出ます。休憩が始まりました。休憩は15分続きます。次は歴史の授業です。私は3階に行く必要があります。歴史の教室はそこです。私は3階へ行き、教室に入

the auditorium. Ten minutes remain before the beginning of the class. I go into the auditorium and sit down on a chair. Sitting next to me is my friend Mike. He gets very good grades. Our teacher comes in. His name is Mr. Steven. He picks up the chalk and writes a topic on the board. Students take out their notebooks and pens. We write down the topic. Mr. Steven then distributes our books on physics. He asks us to open the books on page twelve. We write down formulas and rules in our notebooks. Mr. Steven tells us about the topic. We listen carefully. The class lasts an hour and a half. Then I leave the auditorium. The break has started. The break lasts fifteen minutes. Next is the history lesson. I need to go to the third floor. The history classroom is there. I go up to the third floor and I go into the classroom. Our

ります。　私たちの先生はおりべん先生と言います。彼はてーぶるにつき、新聞を読んでいます。部屋の黒板には大きな地図がかけてあります。
　生徒は彼の部屋に来て、自分たちの席に座ります。授業が始まります。私たちの先生は地図を見ます。彼は私たちにぶりゅっせるの町の歴史を教えます。そして彼は黒板に議題を書きます。授業は1時間半続きます。そして私たちは部屋の外に出ます。長い休憩が始まります。それは30分続きます。私は大学から出てかふぇに行きます。私の友達のまいくは私と一緒に来ます。かふぇは大学の近くに位置します。
　私たちはかふぇに入ります。私はぴざとこーひーと注文します。私はまいくとかふぇの中で20分間滞在します。それから私は食べ物の料金をうぇいたーに払い、そしてかふぇを出ます。3番目の授業は生物学です。私は生物学の授業に行くのが好きです。私たちのいん

teacher is called Mr. Oliven. He is sitting at a table and is reading a newspaper. A large map hangs on the blackboard in his room. Students come to the room and sit down in their seats. The class begins. Our teacher looks at a map. He tells us the history of the city of Brussels. He then writes a topic on the board. The class lasts an hour and a half. Then we go out of the room. The long break begins. It lasts thirty minutes. I go out of the university and go to a cafe. My friend Mike goes with me. The cafe is located nearby. We come into the cafe. I order a pizza and coffee. I sit in the cafe with Mike for twenty minutes. Then I pay the bill for the food to the waiter and leave the cafe. The third lesson is in biology. I love to go to lectures on biology. Our instructor Mr. Christin tells very interesting things. The

すとらくたーのくりすてん先生はとても面白いことを言います。授業は1時間半続きます。それから私は英語の授業に行きます。私は英語が得意です。
私の祖父と祖母はいぎりすに住んでいます。私はよく彼らを訪ねに行きます。私は授業の後に図書館に行こうと考えます。明日地理学のてすとがあるため、私は良く準備をする必要があります。私は世界の海洋についての本を借りたいです。私はその概要を作る必要があります。図書館は私たちの大学にあります。それは4階にあります。私は図書館に行きます。沢山の生徒が図書館で座っています。彼らは読んだりめもを書きとめたりしています。
すでに午後4時です。私は疲れました。そのため私はその本を家へ持ち帰りたいです。
私は司書のところに行きます。私は彼に海洋についての本を見せて欲しいと言います。司書は私に3冊の本を見せます。私は本を見ます。私はそのうち2冊を

lecture lasts an hour and a half. Then I go to the English class. I know English well. My grandparents live in England. I often go to visit them. I think I'll go to the library after classes. Tomorrow I have a test in geography, so I need to prepare well. I want to take a book on the world's oceans. I need to make an outline. The library is located at our university. It is on the fourth floor. I go to the library. A lot of students are sitting in the library. They are reading and taking notes. It's already four o'clock in the afternoon. I'm tired. So I want to take the books home. I go to the librarian. I ask him to show me a book about the oceans. The librarian shows me three books. I look at the books. I decide to take two of them home. I also take a magazine. I check out the books and the magazine.

家に持って帰ることに決めます。私は雑誌も取ります。私は本と雑誌をちぇっくあうとします。司書は私に本と雑誌を3週間以内に返さないといけないと言います。私は本と雑誌を持って家へ帰ります。

The librarian says that I have to return the books and the magazine in three weeks. I take the books and the magazine, and go home.

kyou watashi ha daigaku ni ikimasu. watashi ha sokoni hachiji sanjyuppun ni iru hitsuyou ga arimasu. watashi ha kigaemasu. soto ha atsui node, watashi ha usugi wo shimasu. soshite watashi ha choushoku wo tabemasu. watashi ha choushoku ni sandoicchi wo tabe, soshite koucha wo nomimasu. watashi ha jibun no mono wo atsumemasu. watashi ha no-tobukku, pen, enpitsu, jougi soshite rekishi no kyoukasho wo daigaku ni motte ikimasu. watashi ha ie wo dete basutei ni ikimasu. watashi ha basu ni notte daigaku ni ikimasu. watashi ha daigaku wo mitsukemasu. takusan no seito ga iriguchi ni imasu. watashi ha doa he iki, daigaku ni hairimasu. kyou watashi ha kurasu ga yottsu arimasu. ichibanme no jyugyou ha butsurigaku, nibanme ha rekishi, sanbanme ha seibutsugaku, soshite yonbanme ha eigodesu. watashi ha butsurigaku no tameni kougishitsu ni iku hitsuyou ga arimasu. watashi ha nikai heto kaidan wo agarimasu. watashi ha butsurigaku no kougishitsu he ikimasu. takusan no seito ga kougishitsu no chikaku ni tatteimasu. jugyou ga hajimarumadeni ato jyuppun nokotte imasu. watshi ha kougishitsu ni hairi, isu ni suwarimasu. watashi no tonari ni suwatteiruno ha watashi no tomodachi no maiku desu. kare ha totemo ii seiseki wo torimasu. watashitachi no sensei ga haittekimasu. kare no namae ha suti-bunsensei desu. kare ha cho-ku wo tori, kokuban ni gidai wo kakimasu. seito tachi ha jibun no no-tobukku to pen wo toridashimasu. watashitachi ha gidai wo kakitomemasu. suti-bunsensei ha sorekara watashitachi no butsurigaku no hon wo haifu shimasu. kare ha hon no juni pe-ji wo hirakuyouni iimasu. watashitachi ha suushiki to ru-ru wo no-tobukku ni kakitomemasu. suti-bunsensei ha gidai ni tsuite watashitachi ni hanashimasu. watashitachi ha sore wo chuibukaku kikimasu. jugyou ha ichijikanhan tsudukimasu.soshite watashi ha kougishitsu wo demasu. kyukei ga hajimarimashita. kyukei ha jugofun tsudukimasu. tsugi ha rekishi no jugyou desu. watashi ha sangai ni iku hitsuyou ga arimasu. rekishi no kyoushitsu ha soko desu. watashi ha sangai he iki, kyoushitsu ni hairimasu. watashitachi no sensei ha oribensensei to iimasu. kare ha te-buru ni tsuki, shinbun wo yondeimasu. heya no kokuban niha ookina chizu ga kakete arimasu. seito ha kare no heyani kite, jibuntachi no seki ni suwarimasu. jugyou ga hajimarimasu. watashitachi no sensei ha chizu wo mimasu. kare ha watashitachi ni bryusseru no machi no rekishi wo oshiemasu. soshite kare ha kokuban ni gidai wo kakimasu. jugyou ha ichijikanhan tsudukimasu. soshite watashitachi ha heya no soto ni demasu. nagai kyukei ga hajimarimasu. sanjuppun tsudukimasu. watashi ha

daigaku kara dẹte, kafe ni ikimasu. watashi no tomodachi no maiku ha watashi to issho ni kimasu. kafe ha daigaku no chikakuni ichishimasu. watashitachi ha kafe ni hairimasu. watashi ha piza to ko-hi- wo chumonshimasu. watashi ha maiku to kafe no naka de nijuppunkan taizai shimasu. sorekara watashi ha tabemono no ryoukin wo ueita- ni harai, soshite kafe wo demasu. sanbanme no jugyou ha seibutsugaku desu. watashi ha seibutsugaku no jugyou ni iku noga sukidesu. watashitachi no insutorakuta- no kurisutinsensei ha totemo omoshiroi koto wo iimasu. jugyou ha ichijikanhan tsudukimasu. Sorekara watashi ha eigo no jugyou ni ikimasu. watashi ha eigo ga tokui desu. watashi no sofu to sobo ha igirisu ni sundeimasu. Watashi ha yoku karera wo tazuneni ikimasu. watashi ha jugyou no ato ni toshokanni ikou to kangaemasu. ashita chirigaku no tesuto ga arutame, watashi ha yoku junbi wo suru hitsuyou ga arimasu. watashi ha sekai no kaiyou ni tsuite no hon wo karitaidesu. watashi ha sono gaiyou wo tsukuru hitsuyou ga arimasu. toshokan wa watashitachi no daigaku ni arimasu. sore ha yonkai ni arimasu. watashi ha toshokan ni ikimasu. takusan no seito ga toshokan de suwatte imasu. karera ha yondari memo wo kakitometari shiteimasu. sudeni gogo yojidesu. watashi ha tsukaremashita. sonotame watashi ha sono hon wo ie he mochikaeritaidesu. watashi ha shisho no tokoro ni ikimasu. watashi ha kare ni kaiyou ni tsuite no hon wo misetehoshi to iimasu. shisho ha watashi ni sansatsu no hon wo misemasu. watashi ha hon wo mimasu. watashi ha sonouchi nisatsu wo ie ni motte kaerukotoni kimemasu. watashi ha zasshi mo torimasu. watshi ha hon to zasshi wo chekkuauto shimasu.shisho ha watshi ni hon to zasshi wo sanshukan inai ni kaesanaitoikenai to iimasu. watashi ha hon to zasshi wo motte ie he kaerimasu.

C

質問と答え

-あなたは今日どこに行きますか？
-今日私は大学に行きます。
-あなたは何時にそこにいる必要がありますか？
- 私は8時半にそこにいる必要があります。
-あなたはどうして薄い服を着るのですか？
- 私は外が暑いため薄い服を着ます。

Questions and answers

- Where are you going today?
- Today I'm going to university.
- At what time do you have to be there?
- I have to be there at half past eight.
- Why do you wear light clothing?

—あなたは朝食に何を食べますか？
—私は朝食にさんどいっちを食べ、そして紅茶を飲みます。
—あなたは大学へ何を持っていきますか？
—私はのーとぶっく、ぺん、鉛筆、定規そして歴史の教科書を大学へ持っていきます。
—あなたは歩いて大学に行きますか、それともばすで行きますか？
—私はばすで大学に行きます。
—あなたは今日いくつ授業がありますか？
—私は今日4つ授業があります。
—あなたは何の教科を勉強していますか？
—物理学、歴史、生物学そして英語です。
—あなたは何階に行く必要がありますか？
—私は2階へと階段を上ります。
—あなたは学長の所へ行きますか？
—いいえ、私は物理学の講義室に行きます。

- I wear light clothing because it is hot outside.
- What do you eat for breakfast?
- For breakfast I eat a sandwich and drink tea.
- What do you take with you to university?
- I take a notebook, pen, pencil, ruler and history textbook to university.
- Do you get on foot or by bus to university?
- I get to university by bus.
- How many classes do you have today?
- Today I have four classes.
- What subjects do you study?
- Physics, history, biology and English.
- To which floor do you have to get?
- I climb the stairs to the second floor.
- Do you go to the dean?
- No, I'm going to the physics

- 授業が始まるまでにあと何分残っていますか？
- 授業が始まるまでにあと10分残っています。
- 誰があなたの隣に座っていますか？
- 私の友達のまいくが私の隣に座っています。
- 彼は大学で良い成績を取りますか？
- はい、彼はとても良い成績を取ります。
- あなたの先生の名前は何ですか？
- 彼の名前はすてぃーぶん先生です。
- すてぃーぶん先生の授業はどう始まりますか？
- すてぃーぶん先生は黒板に議題を書きます。
- すてぃーぶん先生は何を配布しますか？
- すてぃーぶん先生は私たちの物理学の本を配布します。
- その本のどのページを開きますか？
- 私たちはその本の12ページを開きます。
- あなたは何をのーとぶっくに書きますか？

auditorium.
- How many minutes are left before the start of classes?
- There are ten minutes before the class.
- Who is sitting next to you?
- My friend Mike is sitting next to me.
- Does he do well at university?
- Yes, he does very well.
- What is the name of your teacher?
- His name is Mr. Steven.
- How does Mr. Steven start class?
- Mr. Steven writes the topic on the board.
- What does Mr. Steven distribute?
- Mr. Steven distributes our books on physics.
- On which page do you open the book?
- We open the book on page twelve.
- What do you write in your

- 私たちは数式とるーるをのーとぶっくに書きます。
- あなたはすてぃーぶん先生の話を注意深く聞きますか？
- はい、私たちは彼の話を注意深く聞きます。
- 授業はどれくらい続きますか？
- 授業は1時間半続きます。
- 休憩はどれくらいの長さですか？
- 休憩は15分続きます。
- 歴史の教室は何階にありますか？
- 歴史の教室は3階にあります。
- あなたの先生の名前は何ですか？
- 私たちの先生の名前はおりべん先生です。
- 彼は休憩中何をしますか？
- 彼はてーぶるにつき、そして新聞をよみます。
- 歴史の教室の黒板には何がかかっていますか？
- 大きな地図が黒板にかけてあります。

- We write formulas and rules in our notebooks.
- Do you listen to Mr. Steven carefully?
- Yes, we listen to him carefully.
- How long does a lesson last?
- A lesson lasts an hour and a half.
- How long is the break?
- Break lasts fifteen minutes.
- On what floor is the history room?
- The history room is on the third floor.
- What is your teacher's name?
- Our teacher's name is Mr. Oliven.
- What does he do during the break?
- He sits at the table and reads a newspaper.
- What hangs on the blackboard in the history notebook?

- 先生はあなたに何を教えますか？
- 彼はぶりゅっせるの町の歴史を教えます。
- 長い休憩の時間はどれくらいの長さですか？
- それは30分続きます。
- 誰があなたとかふぇに行きますか？
- 私の友達のまいくが私と一緒に来ます。
- かふぇは遠いですか？
- いいえ、かふぇは隣です。
- あなたは何を注文しますか？
- 私はぴざとこーひーを注文します。
- あなたはどれくらいの時間かふぇにいますか？
- 私はまいくとかふぇに20分います。
- あなたは誰に食べ物の料金を払いますか？
- 私は食べ物の料金をうぇいたーに払います。
- あなたは生物学の授業は好きですか？
- はい、私は生物学の授業に行くのが好きです。

- A large map hangs on the blackboard.
- What does the teacher tell you about?
- He tells us the history of the city of Brussels.
- How long is the big break?
- It lasts thirty minutes.
- Who goes with you to the cafe?
- My friend Mike goes with me.
- Is the cafe far?
- No, the cafe is next door.
- What do you order?
- I order a pizza and coffee.
- How long do you sit in the cafe?
- I sit in the cafe with Mike for twenty minutes.
- To whom do you pay the bill for the food?
- I pay the bill for the food to the waiter.
- Do you like biology classes?
- Yes, I like to go to biology room?

　　　　　　せんせい　なまえ
-あなたの 先 生 の名 前はくりすてぃんですか？
　　　　かれ　なまえ
-はい、 彼 の名 前はくりすてぃんです。
　　　かれ　　　　　おもしろ　おし
- 彼 はものを 面 白 く 教 えますか？
　　　　わたし　　　　せんせい
-はい、 私 たちの 先 生 のくりすてぃん
せんせい　　　　　　　　おもしろ
先 生 はものをとても 面 白 くします。
　　　　　えいご　はな
-あなたは英 語を話 しますか？
　　　　わたし　えいご　はな
-はい、 私 は英 語を話 します。
　　　　　そふ　そぼ
-あなたの祖父と祖母はどこにいますか？
　　わたし　そふ　そぼ　　　　　　　す
- 私 の祖父と祖母はいぎりすに住んでいます。
　　　　　かれ　　たず　い
-あなたは彼 らを訪 ねに行きますか？
　　　わたし　　　かれ　　たず　い
-はい、 私 はよく彼 らを訪 ねに行きます。
　　　　　じゅぎょう　のち　　い
-あなたは授 業 の後 どこに行きたいですか？
　わたし　としょかん　い　　　おも
- 私 は図 書 館 に行こうと思 います。
　なに　きょうか　あした
- 何 の教 科で明 日てすとがありますか？
　あしたわたし　　　ちりがく
- 明 日 私 は地理学のてすとがあります。
　　　　　　　　　じゅんび　　ひつよう
-あなたはそれのために準 備をする必 要があ
りますか？
　　　　わたし　　　じゅんび　　　ひつよう
-はい、 私 はよく準 備をする必 要 があり
ます。
　　　　　　　なに　しゅるい　ほん　としょかん　か
-あなたは何 の種 類の本を図 書 館 から借

classes.
- Is your teacher's name Mr. Christin?
- Yes, his name is Mr. Christin.
- Does he tells things in an interesting way?
- Yes, our teacher Mr. Christin makes things very interesting.
- Do you speak English?
- Yes, I speak English.
- Where are your grandparents?
- My grandparents live in England.
- Do you go to visit them?
- Yes, I often go to visit them.
- Where do you want to go after classes?
- I think I'll go to the library.
- In what subject do you have a test tomorrow?
- Tomorrow I have a test in geography.
- Do you need to prepare for it?

りたいですか？
- 私は世界の海洋についての本を借りたいです。
- どうしてあなたはそれらの本が必要ですか？
- 私は概要を書く必要があります。
- 図書館はどこですか？
- 図書館は私たちの大学の4階にあります。
- 何人の生徒たちが図書館にいますか？
- 沢山の生徒たちが図書館で座っています。
- 彼らは何をしますか？
- 彼らは読んだりめもを書きとめたりしています。
- あなたは概要を書くために本を取り、そして図書館で座りますか？
- いいえ、私は疲れていますので、本を家に持ち帰りたいです。
- あなたは司書に何を聞きますか？
- 私は彼に海洋についての本を見せて欲しいと言います。
- あなたは何冊の本を家に持ち帰ることを決定しますか？

- Yes, I need to prepare well.
- What kind of books do you want to take out of the library?
- I want to take a book on the world's oceans.
- Why do you need these books?
- I need to write an outline.
- Where is the library?
- The library is in our university on the fourth floor.
- How many students are in the library?
- A lot of students sit in the library.
- What do they do?
- They read and take notes.
- Do you take a book and sit down to write an outline in the library?
- No, I'm tired, so I want to take the books home.
- What do you ask the librarian?
- I ask him to show me a book about oceans.
- How many books do you

- 私(わたし)は2冊(さつ)の本(ほん)を家(いえ)に持(も)ち帰(かえ)ることを決定(けってい)します。

- あなたは雑誌(ざっし)も取(と)りますか？

- はい、私(わたし)は雑誌(ざっし)も取(と)ります。

- あなたはいつ本(ほん)と雑誌(ざっし)を返(かえ)す必要(ひつよう)がありますか？

- 司書(ししょ)は私(わたし)に本(ほん)と雑誌(ざっし)を3週間以内(しゅうかんいない)に返(かえ)す必要(ひつよう)があると言(い)います。

decide to take home?

- I decide to take two books home.

- Do you also take a magazine?

- Yes, I also take a magazine.

- When do you have to return the books and magazine?

- The librarian says that I have to return the books and magazine in three weeks.

15

Audio

氷を砕く
Break the ice

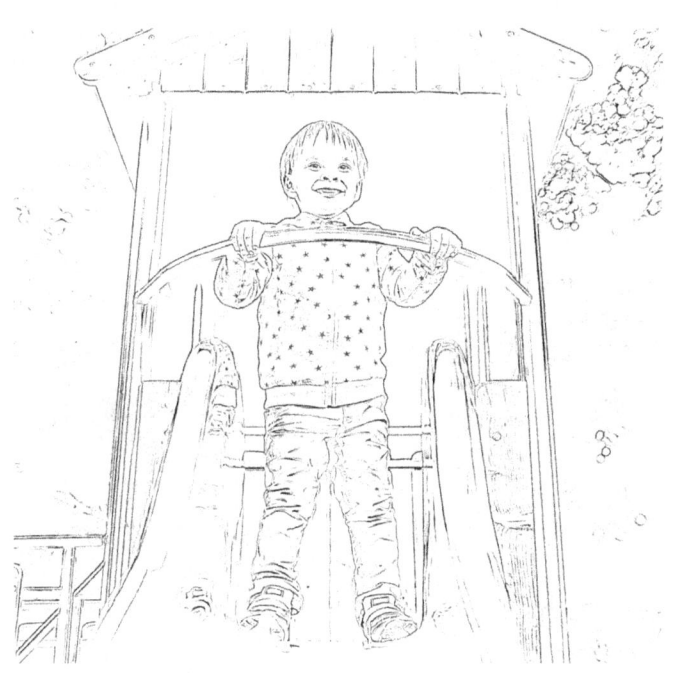

幼(おさな)いロバートは公園(こうえん)で遊(あそ)んでいます。

"ロバート、お家(いえ)に帰(かえ)ってきなさい！"と彼(かれ)のお母さんが言(い)いました。

ロバートはお母さんを見上(みあ)げて"僕(ぼく)は疲(つか)れてるの？"とお母さんに聞(き)きました。

"違(ちが)うわよ、ロバート"

"僕(ぼく)は寒(さむ)いのかな？"

Little Robert is playing on the playground.

"Robert, come home!" his mother calls. Robert looks up at his mom.

"Am I tired?" he asks his mom.

"No, dear," Robert's mom answers.

"Am I cold?" he asks again.

"No, honey. You are hungry," the mom says.

"Okay, mommy! I am

"違うわ、あなたはお腹が減っているの"
"そっか！今帰るよ！"と嬉しそうに言って足早に帰宅した。

osanai Roba-To wa kōen de asondeimasu. Roba-To, oie ni kaetteki nasai! to kare no okāsan ga iimashita. Roba-To wa okāsan o miagete boku wa tsukareteru no? to okāsan ni kikimashita. chigau wa yo, Roba-To boku wa samui no ka na? chigau wa, anata wa onaka ga hetteiru no so ka! ima kaeru yo! to ureshisō ni itte ashibaya ni kitakushita.

coming!" Robert says happily and runs home quickly.

ジャックはアルバイトとして働きたいです
Jack wants to work part-time

A

単語
Words

1. ～になる [～ni naru] - become
2. ～の前、より早く [～no mae, yorihayaku] - before, earlier
3. いっぱい [ippai] - full
4. こんにちは [konnichiha] - hello
5. する、運び出す [suru, hakobidasu] - do, carry out
6. アクティブ [akutibu] - active
7. オランダの [orandano] - Dutch
8. オランダ人 [orandajinno] - Dutchman
9. コマーシャル、広告 [koma-sharu, koukoku] - commercial, advertisement
10. ステータス [sute-tasu] - status
11. ノック [nokku] - knock
12. パートタイム、非常勤 [pa-totaimu, hijoukin] - part-time

13. パートタイムの仕事、アルバイト [pa-totaimuno shigoto, arubaito] - part-time job
14. 運ぶ、抱える [hakobu, kakaeru] - carry
15. 運転免許 [untenmenkyo] - driving license
16. 家族 [kazoku] - family
17. 稼ぐ [kasegu] - earn
18. 荷物を積み込む人、港湾労働者 [nimotsu wo tsumikomuhito, kouwanroudousha] - loader, stevedore
19. 感謝する [kanshasuru] - thanks
20. 願い、したがる [negai, shitagaru] - wish, desire
21. 記入した [kinyuushita] - filled out
22. 記入する [kinyuusuru] - fill out
23. 教育 [kyouiku] - education
24. 経営者、社長 [keieisha, shachou] - manager, head
25. 経験 [keiken] - experience
26. 結婚している [kekkonshiteiru] - married
27. 権利 [kenri] - rights
28. 個人の [kojinno] - personal
29. 仕事 [shigoto] - work
30. 仕事につく [shigotoni tsuku] - get a job
31. 仕事紹介、雇用 [shigotoshoukai, koyou] - placement, employment
32. 自由に、ペラペラに [jiyuuni, peraperani] - free(ly), fluently
33. 質問事項、質問事項表 [shitsumonjikou, shitsumonjikousho] - questionnaire
34. 社交的な [shakoutekina] - sociable
35. 収まる [osamaru] - settle
36. 女の子、（女性）[onnanoko, josei] - girl
37. 人 [hito] - person
38. 男性 [dansei] - male
39. 提案する、提供する [teiansuru, teikyousuru] - suggest, offer
40. 電話 [denwa] - phone
41. 肉体労働 [nikutairoudou] - physical work
42. 年齢 [nenrei] - age
43. 能力、スキル [nouryoku, sukiru] - skill
44. 苗字 [myouji] - last name
45. 名前 [namae] - name
46. 約束 [yakusoku] - promise

B

じゃっくはお金を少ししか持っていません。彼はあるばいととして働きたいと考えています。彼は大学の授業の後自由時間があります。

Jack has little money. He wants to work part-time. He has free time after university classes.

彼の友達のまいくは荷物を積み込む人として学校の後すーぱーで働いています。まいくは1日30ゆーろ受け取ります。じゃっくはまいくにどうやって仕事を見つけたか聞きます。まいくはじゃっくに、彼は職業紹介所に行ったと言います。そこで彼はその仕事を提供されました。まいくはじゃっくに紹介所の住所を渡します。じゃっくも職業紹介所に行くことを決めます。紹介所は町の中央に位置します。じゃっくはそこに地下鉄で行きます。彼はすぐに紹介所を見つけます。学生のための仕事の広告が沢山入口にかかっています。じゃっくは中に入ります。そこで彼は長い列を見ます。これらの人々も仕事が欲しいと考えています。彼らはへるぷですくに立っています。人々は個人情報のための質問事項に答えています。じゃっくは列に並びます。じゃっくの番が15分でき来ます。

jakku ha okane wo sukoshi shika motteimasen. kare ha arubaito toshite hatarakitai to kangaete imasu. kare ha daigaku no jugyou no ato jiyuujikan ga arimasu. kare no tomodachi no maiku ha nimotsu wo tsumikomu hito toshite gakkou no ato su-pa- de hataraite imasu. maiku ha ichinichi sanju yu-ro uketorimasu. jakku ha maiku ni douyatte shigoto wo mitsuketaka kikimasu. maiku ha jakku ni, kare ha shokugyoushoukaijo ni itta to iimasu. sokode kare ha sono shigoto wo teikyou saremashita. maiku ha jakku ni shoukaijo

His friend Mike works as a loader in a supermarket after school. Mike gets thirty euros per day. Jack asks Mike how he found the job. Mike tells Jack that he went to an employment agency. There he was offered the job. Mike gives Jack the address of the agency. Jack also decides to go to the employment agency. The agency is located in the city center. Jack gets there by subway. He quickly finds the agency. A lot of ads about work for students hangs at the entrance. Jack goes inside. There he sees a long queue. These are people who also want to get a job. They stand at the help desk. People take

no juusho wo watashimasu. jakku mo shokugyoushoukaijo ni ikukoto wo kimemasu. shoukaijo ha machi no chuou ni ichishimasu. jakku ha soko ni chikatetsu de ikimasu. kare ha suguni shoukaijo wo mitsukemasu. gakusei no tameno shigoto no koukoku ga takusan iriguchi ni kakatte imasu. jakku ha naka ni hairimasu. sokode kare ha nagai retsu wo mimasu. korera no hitobito mo shigoto ga hoshii to kangaeteimasu. karera ha herupudesuku ni tatteimasu. hitobito ha kojinjouhou no tameno shitsumonjikou ni kotaeteimasu. jakku ha retsu ni narabimasu. jakku no ban ga juugofun de kimasu.

"こんにちは、私の名前はりさです。"へるぷですくの女性がじゃっくに言います。"konnichiha, watashi no namae ha risa desu." herupudesuku no josei ga jakku ni iimasu.

"こんにちは、私はじゃっくです。"じゃっくは言います。"konnichiha, watashi ha jakku desu." jakku ha iimasu.

"あなたは仕事を探していますか？"女性が彼に聞きます。"anata ha shigoto wo sagashite imasuka?" josei ga kare ni kikimasu.

"はい。"じゃっくは言います。"hai." jakku ha iimasu.

"あなたはふるたいむとして働きたいですか、それともあるばいととして働きたいですか？"女性が聞きます。"anata ha furutaimu toshite hatarakitaidesuka, soretomo arubaito toshite hatarakitaidesuka?" josei ga kikimasu.

"私は学生で、授業の後に働きたいです。"じゃっくは言います。"watashi ha gakusei de, jugyou no ato ni hatarakitaidesu." jakku ha iimasu.

"それでは学生のための質問事項表の記入を完了させてください。質問事項表の記入が完了したら、部門長の所にそれを持って行ってください。"

questionnaires for personal data. Jack stands in the line. Jack's turn comes in fifteen minutes.

"Hello, my name is Lisa," says the girl at the help desk to Jack.

"Hello, I am Jack," Jack says.

"Are you looking for work?" the girl asks him.

"Yes," Jack says.

"Do you want to work full-time or part-time?" the girl asks.

"I am a student and I want to work after classes," Jack says.

"Then take and complete the questionnaire for students, please. When you complete the questionnaire, take it to the head of

女性は言い、彼に質問事項表を渡します。 "soredeha gakusei no tameno shitsumonjikouhyou no kinyuu wo kanryou sasetekudasai. Shitsumonjikouhyou no kinyuu ga kanryoushitara, bumonchou no tokoro ni sore wo motteitte kudasai." josei ha ii, kare ni shitsumonjikouhyou wo watashimasu.

"ありがとう。"じゃっくは言い、そして女性から質問事項表を受け取ります。 "arigatou." jakku ha ii, soshite josei kara shitsumonjikouhyou wo uketorimasu.

じゃっくはぺんを取り、そして質問事項に答えます。 jakku ha pen wo tori, soshite shitsumonjikou ni kotaemasu.

名前：じゃっく
namae: jakku

苗字：すとろーまん
myouji: sutoro-man

性別：男性
seibetsu: dansei

年齢：19才
nenrei: juukyuusai

国籍：おらんだ
kokuseki: oranda

結婚歴：独身
kekkonreki: dokushin

教育：私はてくのろじーとでざいんの大学で勉強しています。
kyouiku: watashi ha tekunoroji- to dezain no daigaku de benkyou shiteimasu.

前職：私は働いたことがありません。
zenshoku: watashi ha hataraitakoto ga arimasen.

department," the girl says and gives him a questionnaire.

"Thank you," Jack says and takes the form.

Jack picks up a pen and fills out the questionnaire.

Name: Jack

Surname: Stroman

Gender: Male

Age: Nineteen years old

Nationality: Dutch

Marital status: Single

Education: I study at the University of Technology and Design.

Previous work: I have not worked before.

What skills and experience do you have?: I am an active

どのような能力と経験を持っていますか？：
私は活発で社交的です。私は肉体労働ができます。私はこんぴゅーたーを使った仕事もできます。
donoyouna nouryoku to keiken wo motteimasuka?: watashi ha kappatsu de shakouteki desu. watashi ha nikutairoudou ga dekimasu. watashi ha konpyu-ta- wo tsukatta shigoto mo dekimasu.

言語(0:無、10:堪能)：英語7、どいつ語10、おらんだ語10
gengo(0-nashi 10-tannou): eigo 7, doitsugo 10, orandago 10

運転免許：なし
untenmenkyo: nashi

期待する給料：1日30-40ゆーろ
kitaisuru kyuryou: ichinichi 30-40yu-ro

電話番号：+3456787487
denwabangou: +3456787487

じゃっくはそのふぉーむを持ち、そして部門長のおふぃすへいきます。彼はのっくをしておふぃすに入ります。
jakku ha sono fo-mu wo mochi, soshite bumonchou no ofisu he ikimasu. kare ha nokku wo shite ofisu ni hairimasu.

"こんにちは、私の名前はじゃっくです。私は部門長に私の質問事項表を渡すように言われました。"じゃっくはですくにいる女性に言います。
"konnichiha, watashi no namae ha jakkudesu. watashiha bumonchou ni watashi no shitsumonjikouhyou wo watasuyouni iwaremashita." jakku ha desuku ni iru josei ni iimasu.

and sociable person. I can do physical work. I can also do work on the computer.

Languages (0: no, 10: fluent): English 7, German 10, Dutch 10

Driving license: No

Salary expectations: 30-40 euro per day

Phone number: +3456787487

Jack takes the form and goes to the office of the head of department. He knocks and comes into the office.

"Hello, my name is Jack. I was told to give the head of the department my questionnaire," Jack says to the woman sitting at the desk.

"Hello, my name is Eva Steg. I am the head of this department. You

"こんにちは、私の名前はえば・すてぐです。私は部門長です。あなたの質問事項表を私に渡してください。"彼女は答えます。
"konnichiha, watashi no namae ha eba・sutegu desu. watashi ha bumonchou desu. anata no shitsumonjikouhyou wo watashi ni watashitekudasai." kanojo ha kotaemasu.

"はいどうぞ。"質問事項表を渡しながら、じゃっくは言います。"いつ仕事をもらえますか？"
"hai douzo."shitsumonjikouhyou wo watashinagara, jakku ha iimasu. "itsu shigoto wo moraemasuka?"

"私たちがあなたのための仕事を見つけたら、あなたに電話します。"彼女は言います。
"watashitachi ga anatano tameno shigoto wo mitsuketara, anata ni denwashimasu." kanojo ha iimasu.

can give me your questionnaire," she answers.

"Here you are," Jack says, handing over his questionnaire. "When can I get a job?"

"We will call you when we find a job for you," she says.

C

質問と答え

-じゃっくは沢山お金を持っていますか？
-いいえ、じゃっくはお金を少ししか持っていません。
-じゃっくは仕事が欲しいですか？
-はい、彼はお金を稼ぎたいです。
-彼はあるばいとのための時間はありますか？
-はい、彼は大学の授業の後に自由時間があります。

Questions and answers

- Does Jack have a lot of money?

- No, Jack has little money.

- Does Jack want to get a job?

- Yes, he wants to earn money.

- Does he have time for part-time work?

- Yes, he has free time after

- 彼の友達のまいくは何をしていますか？
- 彼の友達のまいくは荷を積み込む人として、学校の後すーぱーで働いています。
- まいくはいくらもらいますか？
- まいくは1日30ゆーろもらいます。
- じゃっくはまいくにどこでその仕事を見つけたか聞きますか？
- はい、まいくはじゃっくに仕事紹介所の住所を渡します。
- この紹介所はどこですか？
- その紹介所は町の中央に位置します。
- じゃっくはそこにばすで行きますか？
- いいえ、じゃっくはそこに地下鉄で行きます。
- じゃっくは紹介所の入り口で何を見ますか？
- 学生のための仕事の広告が沢山入口にかかっています。
- 紹介所には沢山人がいますか？
- はい、そこで彼は長い列を見ます。

university classes.

- What does his friend Mike do?

- His friend Mike works as a loader in a supermarket after university classes.

- How much money does Mike get?

- Mike gets thirty euros per day.

- Does Jack ask Mike where he found the job?

- Yes, Mike gives Jack address of an employment agency.

- Where is this agency?

- The agency is located in the city center.

- Does Jack go there by bus?

- No, Jack gets there by subway.

- What does Jack see at the entrance to the agency?

- Many ads about work for students are hanging at the entrance.

- Are there many people at

- この人々は誰ですか？
- この人々も仕事が欲しいと考えています。
- 人々は何に答えていますか？
- 人々は個人情報の質問事項に答えています。
- じゃっくはどれくらいの時間列に並んでいますか？
- じゃっくは列に15分並びます。
- じゃっくはふるたいむとして働きたいですか、それともあるばいととして働きたいですか？
- じゃっくは大学生で、授業の後に働きたいと考えています。
- じゃっくは誰に完了した質問事項表を渡しますか？
- じゃっくはふぉーむを部門長に渡します。
- どれくらい早くじゃっくは仕事をもらえますか？
- 彼らはじゃっくのための仕事を見つけたら彼に電話すると約束します。

the agency?
- Yes, there he sees a long line.
- Who are these people?
- These are people who also want to get a job.
- What do people take?
- People take personal questionnaires.
- How much time does Jack stand in the line?
- Jack stands in the line for fifteen minutes.
- Does Jack want to work full-time or part-time?
- Jack is a university student and wants to work after classes.
- To whom does Jack give the completed application form?
- Jack gives the form to the head of the department.
- How soon can Jack get a job?
- They promise to call Jack when they find a job for him.

日英辞書
Japanese-English dictionary

10、十 [juu, juu] - ten
12、十二 [juuni, juuni] - twelve
12番目 [juunibanme] - twelfth
13、十三 [juusan, juusan] - thirteen
15、十五 [juugo, juugo] - fifteen
18、十八 [juuhachi, juuhachi] - eighteen
19、十九 [juukyuu, juukyuu] - nineteen
1、一 [ichi, ichi] - one
1個半 [ikkohan] - one and a half
20、二十 [nijuu, nijuu] - twenty
2、二 [ni, ni] - two
2番 [niban] - second
300、三百 [sanbyaku] - three hundred
3、三 [san, san] - three
3番 [sanban] - third
40、四十 [yonjuu, yonjuu] - forty
4、四 [yon, yon] - four
4番 [yonban] - fourth
5、五 [go, go] - five
6、六 [roku, roku] - six
7、七 [nana, nana] - seven
800、八百 [happyaku, happyakua] - eight hundred
8、八 [hachi, hachi] - eight
9、九 [kyuu, kyuu] - nine
〜なので、だから、それによって [〜nanode, dakara, soreniyotte] - so, because of this
〜かどうか、もし [〜kadouka, moshi] - whether, if
〜から、〜の外へ [〜kara, 〜no sotohe] - from, out of
〜がかかる、値段 [〜ga kakaru, nedan] - cost
〜ごろ [〜goro] - around
〜するため [〜surutame] - in order to, so that
〜だけ、ただ [〜dake, tada] - only, just
〜で、〜の近くで、〜のそばで [〜de, 〜no chikakude, 〜no sobade] - at, near
〜である [〜de aru] - be
〜でない [〜denai] - not
〜と一緒に [〜to isshoni] - with
〜にある、〜がある [〜ni aru, 〜ga aru] - there is, there are
〜にある、〜の中 [〜ni aru, 〜no naka] - in
〜になる [〜ninaru] - become
〜に位置する、〜にある [〜ni ichisuru, 〜niaru] - be (located)
〜に沿って [〜ni sotte] - along
〜に入る [〜ni hairu] - go into
〜のため、〜にとって [〜notame, 〜nitotte] - for
〜の下 [〜no shita] - under
〜の近く、〜のそば [〜no chikaku, no soba] - near
〜の後 [〜no ato] - after
〜の後ろ、〜のため [〜no ushiro, 〜no tame] - behind, for
〜の向かいに [〜no mukaini] - across from
〜の上 [〜no ue] - on
〜の前、より早く [〜no mae, yorihayaku] - before, earlier
〜の方へ [〜no houhe] - towards
〜へ [〜he] - to
〜へ運送する [〜he unsousuru] - transport
〜まで [〜made] - until, to
〜も [〜mo] - also, too
〜を聞く [〜wo kiku] - listen to
あげる、渡す [ageru, watasu] - give
あなた [anata] - you

あなたの [anatano] - your(s)
あれ [are] - that
いいえ;〜は(が)ない [iie, 〜ha(ga) nai] - no; there isn't, there aren't
いくつか、いくらか [ikutsuka, ikuraka] - any, some
いちご [ichigo] - strawberry
いっぱい [ippai] - full
いつ [itsu] - when
いつも [itsumo] - always
うるさい [urusai] - noisy
うるさく [urusaku] - noisily
おいしい [oishii] - tasty
おおよそ [ooyoso] - roughly, approximately
おそらく [osoraku] - probably
お金 [okane] - money
お父さん [otousan] - father
お米 [okome] - rice
かける(電話を) [kakeru(denwa wo)] - call (by phone)
かける、かかる、つるさがる [kakeru, kakaru, tsurusagaru] - hang
かびん [kabin] - vase
かもしれない [kamoshirenai] - maybe
かわいい、美しい [kawaii, utsukushii] - pretty, beautiful
きゅうり [kyuuri] - cucumber
きれい、きれいにする、かたづける [kirei, kireinisuru, katazukeru] - clean, tidy up
ここ [koko] - here
ここ(方向) [koko (houkou)] - here (direction)
このように、なので [konoyouni, nanode] - like this, so
これ [kore] - this
これら(複数) [korera (fukusuu)] - these (plural)
こんにちは [konnichiwa] - hi, hello
さよならを言う [sayonara wo iu] - say goodbye
さらに遠く [saranitooku] - further
しかし・けれども、〜の間、そして [shikashi, keredomo, 〜no aida, soshite] - but, while, and
しなければならない、せざるをえない [shinakerebanaranai, sezaruwoenai] - have to, be obliged
すぐに [suguni] - right away
すでに [sudeni] - already
すべて [subete] - all
する、運び出す [suru, hakobidasu] - do, carry out
そう遠くない [soutookunai] - not far
そう遠くない昔、最近 [soutookunaimukashi, saikin] - not long ago, recently
そこ [soko] - there (place)
そして、後で [soshite, atode] - and, then, later
そちら(の方向) [sochira(no houkou)] - there (direction)
その後、そして [sonoato, soshite] - afterwards, then
たんす、箱 [tansu, hako] - drawer, box
だんろ [danro] - fireplace
つかむ、運転する、輸送する [tsukamu, untensuru, yusousuru] - grab / take by, drive, transport
できる、することができる [dekiru, surukotoga dekiru] - be able to, can
とても [totemo] - very
どうして [doushite] - why
どうやって [douyatte] - how
どこ [doko] - where
どこへ [dokohe] - where to
どれ、何 [dore, nani] - which, what
どれくらい、いくら [dorekurai, ikura] - how much
なぜ、どうして [naze, doushite] - why

なぜなら [nazenara] - because
にわとり、チキン [niwatori, chikin] - chicken
ぬくもりのある、心地の良い [nukumorinoaru, kokochinoyoi] - cozy, comfortable
ねこ [neko] - cat
のどが渇く [nodoga kawaku] - thirty
の間 [no aida] - between
の間に [no aidani] - among
の上、に沿って [no ue, ni sotte] - over, along
の隣に、近く [no tonarini, chikaku] - next to, near
はい [hai] - yes
はかり [hakari] - scales
ばかげたこと、キィエルバサ、ソーセージ [bakagetakoto, kiierubasa, so-se-ji] - baloney, kielbasa, sausage
ふっとうする [futtousuru] - boil
ぶどう [budou] - grape(s)
まくら [makura] - pillow
または [mataha] - or
まもなく [mamonaku] - soon
もちろん [mochiron] - of course
もっと、よりおおくの、まだ [motto, yoriookuno, mada] - more, still
もも [momo] - peach
やく [yaku] - about
ゆでる、いれる [yuderu, ireru] - boil, brew
よく [yoku] - often
りんご [ringo] - apple
を除いて [wo nozoite] - without
を乗せる [wo noseru] - put on
を占める [wo shimeru] - occupy
を通り過ぎる、近く [wo toorisugiru, chikaku] - past, near
アームチェア [a-muchea] - armchair
アイスクリーム [aisukuri-mu] - ice cream
アクティブ [akutibu] - active
アドレス、住所 [adoresu, juusho] - address
アナウンス [anaunsu] - announcement, ad
アパート [apa-to] - apartment, flat
アルコールの [aruko-runo] - alcoholic
イギリス [igirisu] - England
イギリスの女性 [igirisuno josei] - Englishwoman
イタリア [itaria] - Italy
イタリア人 [itariajin] - Italian (person)
ウェイター [ueita-] - waiter
エージェント [e-jento] - agent
エリア、地域 [eria, chiiki] - area, site
エレベーター [erebe-ta-] - elevator
オーナー [o-na-] - owner
オフィス、事務所 [ofisu, jimusho] - office
オランダの [orandano] - Dutch
オランダ人 [orandajinno] - Dutchman
オレンジ [orenji] - orange
カート [ka-to] - wagon, cart
カーペット [ka-petto] - carpet
カップボード、たんす、本棚 [kappubo-do, tansu] - cupboard, wardrobe, bookcase
カフェ [kafe] - cafe
ガス [gasu] - gas
ガラス [garasu] - glass
ガレージ、車庫 [gare-ji, shako] - garage
キー、鍵 [ki-, kagi] - key
キオスク [kiosuku] - kiosk
キッチン [kicchin] - kitchen
キャベツ [kyabetsu] - cabbage
クッキー [kukki-] - cookie
クラブ [kurabu] - club
クリニック [kurinikku] - clinic

グレー [gure-] - gray
ケーキ、デザート [ke-ki, deza-to] - cake, dessert
ゲーム [ge-mu] - game
ゲスト [gesuto] - guest
コーヒー [ko-hi-] - coffee
コーヒーテーブル [ko-hi-te-buru] - coffee table
コーヒーメーカー [ko-hi-me-ka-] - coffeemaker
コインランドリー [koinrandori-] - laundromat, launderette
コップ [koppu] - cup
コマーシャル、広告 [koma-sharu, koukoku] - commercial, advertisement
コメディー [komedi-] - comedy
コレクション [korekushon] - collection
コンサルタント [konsarutanto] - consultant
コンピューター [konpyu-ta-] - computer
ゴミ、生ごみ [gomi, namagomi] - trash, garbage
ゴム [gomu] - rubber
サーモン [sa-mon] - salmon
サッカー [sakka-] - soccer
サッカー選手 [sakka-senshu] - soccer player
サラ [sara] - Sarah
サワークリーム [sawa-kuri-mu] - sour cream
サンドイッチ [sandoicchi] - sandwich
シェイクスピア [sheikusupia] - Shakespeare
シャワー [shawa-] - shower
シャンデリア [shanderia] - chandelier
シリアル [shiriaru] - flakes, cereal
シンク [sinku] - sink
ジュース [ju-su] - juice
スーパー [su-pa-] - supermarket

スープ [su-pu] - soup
スイッチ [suicchi] - switch
スイッチを入れる [suicchi wo ireru] - turn on
スキャン [sukyan] - scan
スタート [suta-to] - start
スタンド [sutando] - stand
スタンプ [sutanpu] - stamp
ステータス [sute-tasu] - status
ステップ [suteppu] - step
ストーブ [suto-bu] - stove
スプーン [supu-n] - spoon
スペイン人 [supeinjin] - Spaniard
ソースパン [so-supan] - saucepan
ソーセージ [so-se-ji] - sausage
ソファー、カウチ [sofa-, kauchi] - sofa, couch
タオル [taoru] - towel
タクシー [takushi-] - taxi
ダイニングルーム [daininguru-mu] - dining room
チーズ [chi-zu] - cheese
チキン [chikin] - chickens
チケット [chiketto] - ticket
チューリップ [chu-rippu] - tulip
チョーク [cho-ku] - chalk
ツアー客 [tsua-kyaku] - tourist
テーブル [te-buru] - table
テーブルクロス [te-burukurosu] - tablecloth
ティーポット [ti-potto] - teapot
テクノロジー [tekunoroji-] - technology
テスト [tesuto] - test
テレビセット [terebisetto] - Tv-set
データ、情報 [de-ta, jouhou] - data, information
ディスプレイ、陳列する [disupurei, chinretsusuru] - display, set out
デザイン [dezain] - design
トースター [to-suta-] - toaster

トイレ、バスルーム [toire, basuru-mu] - toilet, bathroom
トマト [tomato] - tomato
トロリーバス [torori-basu] - trolleybus
トンネル [tonneru] - tunnel
ドア [doa] - door
ドイツの [doitsuno] - German
ドライバー、運転手 [doraiba-, untenshu] - driver
ドライヤー [doraiya-] - dryer
ドラッグストア [doraggusutoa] - drugstore
ナイフ [naifu] - knife
ナプキン [napukin] - napkin
ナポリ [napori] - Naples
ニンジン [ninjin] - carrot
ノートブック [notobukku] - notebook, copybook
ノック [nokku] - knock
ハチミツ [hachimitsu] - honey
ハンドバック、バック [handobakku, bakku] - purse, bag
ハンドル [handoru] - handle
ハンバーガー [hanba-ga-] - hamburger
バー [ba-] - bar
バイク、オートバイ [baiku, o-tobai] - motorcycle, motorbike
バス [basu] - bus
バスケット [basuketto] - basket
バスケットボール [basukettobo-ru] - basketball
バスタブ [basutabu] - bathtub
バスルーム [basuru-mu] - bathroom
バナナ [banana] - banana
バラ [bara] - rose
パートタイム、非常勤 [pa-totaimu, hijoukin] - part-time
パートタイムの仕事、アルバイト [pa-totaimuno shigoto, arubaito] - part-time job
パイナップル [painappuru] - pineapple
パス [pasu] - pass
パスタ、マカロニ [pasuta, makaroni] - pasta, macaroni
パスポート [pasupo-to] - passport
パッケージ [pakke-ji] - package
パパ [papa] - Dad
パン [pan] - bread
ビーチ、砂浜、(川辺の)浜 [bi-chi, (kawabeno)hama] - beach
ピザ [piza] - pizza
フィルム [firumu] - film
フォーク [fo-ku] - fork
フライト、飛行 [furaito, hikou] - flight
フランク [furanku] - Frank
フランス語 [furansugo] - French
ブラシ [burashi] - brush
ブリュッセル [buryusseru] - Brussels
ブレンダー [burenda-] - blender
プラスチック [purasuchikku] - plastic
ベージュ [be-ju] - beige
ベッド [beddo] - bed
ベル、リング [beru, ringu] - bell, ring
ページ [pe-ji] - page
ペア [pea] - pair
ホテル [hoteru] - hotel
ボトル [botoru] - bottle
ポテトチップス [potetochippusu] - potato chips
ポリエチレン、プラスチック [poriechiren, purasuchikku] - polyethylene, plastic
マッシュルーム、きのこ [masshuru-mu, kinoko] - mushroom
ママ [mama] - Mom
ミキサー [mikisa-] - mixer
ミニバス [minibasu] - minibus
メカニック [mekanikku] - mechanic
メトロ、地下鉄 [metoro, chikatetsu] - metro, subway

ユーロ [yu-ro] - Euro
ライター、作家、記者 [raita-, sakka, kisha] - writer
ラジオ [rajio] - radio
ラック、スタンド [rakku, sutando] - rack, stand
ラップトップ [rapputoppu] - laptop
ランプ [ranpu] - lamp
リットル [rittoru] - liter
リビングルーム [ribinguru-mu] - living room
ルール [ru-ru] - rule
レシート [reshi-to] - receipt
レストラン [resutoran] - restaurant
レモン [remon] - lemon
ロールパン、コッペパン、バン [ro-rupan, koppepan, ban] - bread roll, bun
愛、愛する、好き [ai, aisuru, suki] - love
安い [yasui] - inexpensive
暗い [kurai] - dark
案内する、運転する [annaisuru, untensuru] - lead, drive
椅子 [isu] - chair
違う、様々な [chigau, samazamana] - different, various
医者、医師 [isha, ishi] - doctor, physician
育つ、大きくなる [sodatsu, ookikunaru] - grow
育児室 [takujishitsu] - nursery
一週間 [ichishuukan] - week
一緒に [isshoni] - together
一人の、一人用のスペース [hitorino, hitoriyouno supe-su] - single, with space for one person
一生懸命働く [isshoukenmei hataraku] - work hard
一片 [ippen] - piece

一覧、概要 [ichiran, gaiyou] - synopsis, outline
引っ越す(住所を変える) [hikkosu (juusho wo kaeru)] - move (to change address)
飲む [nomu] - drink
右に [migini] - on the right
雨 [ame] - rain
運ぶ、抱える [hakobu, kakaeru] - carry
運転して出て行く [untenshite deteiku] - drive out
運転する、運送する [untensuru, unsousuru] - drive, transport
運転免許 [untenmenkyo] - driving license
映画館 [eigakan] - cinema, movie theater
泳ぐ [oyogu] - swim
英語 [eigo] - English
英国 [eikoku] - Great Britain
駅 [eki] - station
遠く、長い距離の [tooku, nagaikyorino] - far (away), at a long distance
鉛筆 [enpitsu] - pencil
汚い [kitanai] - dirty
横になっている [yokoninatteiru] - lie
黄色 [kiiro] - yellow
屋根 [yane] - roof
温める [atatameru] - warm (up)
何 [nani] - what
何か [nanika] - something
何年 [nannen] - how many years
何年も [nannenmo] - years
価値、価格、値段 [kachi, kakaku, nedan] - value, price
可能な、できる [kanouna, dekiru] - possible
家、家庭 [ie, katei] - house/home
家で [iede] - at home

家へ帰る道 [ie he kaerumichi] - homeward
家具 [kagu] - furniture
家族 [kazoku] - family
果物 [kajitsu] - fruit
稼ぐ [kasegu] - earn
花 [hana] - flower
荷車 [niguruma] - wagon, carriage
荷物 [nimotsu] - baggage
荷物を積み込む人、港湾労働者 [nimotsu wo tsumikomuhito, kouwanroudousha] - loader, stevedore
会う [au] - meet
会計、レジ [kaikei, reji] - checkout, cash register
会計係 [kaikeigakari] - cashier, teller
回(数) [kai(suu)] - time(s) (as in "how many times")
壊す [kowasu] - break
海 [umi] - ocean, sea
開く、開ける [hiraku, akeru] - open
開始 [kaishi] - start
階 [kai] - floor, storey
階段 [kaidan] - staircase
外 [soto] - outside
角 [kado] - corner
革 [kawa] - leather
学校 [gakkou] - school
学長室 [gakuchoushitsu] - dean's office
寒い [samui] - cold
感じる、調子 [kanjiru, choushi] - feel
感謝する [kanshasuru] - thanks
甘い [amai] - sweet
間に合う、〜が十分 [maniau, 〜ga juubun] - be enough
丸い [marui] - round
岸 [kishi] - shore
眼鏡 [megane] - glasses
願い、したがる [negai, shitagaru] - wish, desire

期間 [kikan] - period
機械 [kikai] - machine
気を付ける、注意する [ki wo tsukeru, chuuisuru] - careful
記入した [kinyuushita] - filled out
記入する [kinyuusuru] - fill out
記念碑 [kinenhi] - memorial, monument
起きる / 起き上がる [okiru / okiagaru] - get up, wake up
輝く [kagayaku] - shine
議題、もの、物事 [gidai, mono, monogoto] - subject, thing
丘、山 [oka, yama] - hill, mountain
休む、リラックス [yasumu, rirakkusu] - rest, relax
休暇 [kyuuka] - vacation
急いで [isoide] - quickly
泣く [naku] - cry
牛乳 [gyuunyuu] - milk
拒否する、断る [kyohisuru, kotowaru] - refuse
魚 [sakana] - fish
教える [oshieru] - teach
教育 [kyouiku] - education
教科書、テキスト [kyoukasho, tekisuto] - textbook
橋 [hashi] - bridge
鏡 [kagami] - mirror
近く [chikaku] - near
近づく [chikazuku] - approach
近所 [kinjo] - neighbor
金属 [kinzoku] - metal
金曜日 [kinyoubi] - Friday
銀行 [ginkou] - bank
空 [kara] - empty
兄弟 [kyoudai] - brother
契約する [keiyakusuru] - enter into a contract
経営者、社長 [keieisha, shachou] - manager, head

経験 [keiken] - experience
警察 [keisatsu] - police
警察官 [keisatsukan] - policeman
劇場 [gekijou] - theater
決定、決断 [kettei, ketsudan] - decision
決定する [ketteisuru] - decide
結婚している [kekkonshiteiru] - married
月 [tsuki] - month
権利 [kenri] - rights
犬 [inu] - dog
見せる [miseru] - show
見つける [mitsukeru] - find
見る [miru] - see
現金 [genkin] - cash
言う、教える [iu, oshieru] - tell
言語/言葉 [gengo/ kotoba] - language / tongue
個人の [kojinno] - personal
古い [furui] - old
湖 [mizuumi] - lake
雇用、仕事、職 [koyou, shigoto, shoku] - employment, job
光 [hikari] - light
公園 [kouen] - park
好き、好む [suki, konomu] - like, appeal
広い [hiroi] - spacious
紅茶 [koucha] - tea
考える、思う [kangaeru, omou] - think
行く/乗って行く [iku/ notteiku] - go/ride away
行く、散歩をする、歩く [iku, sanpo wo suru, aruku] - go, walk
行動する、〜する [koudousuru, 〜suru] - act, work
講義室、教室 [kougishitsu, kyoushitsu] - auditorium, class-room
郊外 [kougai] - suburb
高い [takai] - expensive, high
高くない [takakunai] - not tall

高速道路、ハイウェイ [kousokudouro, haiwei] - highway
国 [kuni] - country
国籍 [kokuseki] - nationality
国民 [kokumin] - national
黒 [kuro] - black
黒板 [kokuban] - board
今 [ima] - now
今日 [kyou] - today
左に [hidarini] - on the left
砂糖 [satou] - sugar
座る [suwaru] - sit, sit down
財布 [saifu] - wallet
作る [tsukuru] - make
雑誌 [zasshi] - magazine
皿、プレート [sara, pure-to] - dish, plate
散歩をする [sanpo wo suru] - take a walk
産まれる [umareru] - be born
賛成する [sanseisuru] - agree
残される、残る [nokosareru, nokoru] - be left, stay
仕事 [shigoto] - work
仕事につく [shigotoni tsuku] - get a job
仕事紹介、雇用 [shigotoshoukai, koyou] - placement, employment
司書 [shisho] - librarian
始まり [hajimari] - beginning
始めから [hajimekara] - from the beginning
始めに、1番 [hajimeni, ichiban] - first
姉妹 [shimai] - sister
子供 [kodomo] - child
指し示された [sashishimesareta] - indicated
指し示す [sashishimesu] - indicate
止まる [tomaru] - stop
私 [watashi] - I
私たち [watashitachi] - us, we

私たちの [watashitachino] - our(s)
私の(私の物) [watashino (watashinomono)] - my (mine)
紙 [kami] - paper
紫 [murasaki] - purple
歯 [ha] - teeth , tooth
歯医者 [haisha] - dentist
似ている(に) [niteiru(ni)] - look like
持ってくる、運ぶ [mottekuru, hakobu] - bring, carry
持つ、所有する、飼う [motsu, shoyuusuru, kau] - have, own
時々、いつか [tokidoki, itsuka] - sometime / sometimes, some day
時間 [jikan] - hour , time
次の、次 [tsugino, tsugi] - following, next
治療 [chiryou] - treatment
治療してもらう [chiryoushitemorau] - get treated
自動車、車 [jidousha, kuruma] - automobile, car
自分の体を洗う [jibunno karada wo arau] - wash oneself
自由、タダ [jiyuu, tada] - free
自由に、ペラペラに [jiyuuni, peraperani] - free(ly), fluently
質問事項、質問事項表 [shitsumonjikou, shitsumonjikousho] - questionnaire
写真、絵 [shashin, e] - photograph, picture
写真を撮る [shashin wo toru] - take photos/pictures
社交的な [shakoutekina] - sociable
車のサービス [kurumano sa-bisu] - car service
蛇口、栓 [jaguchi, sen] - faucet, tap
取っ手 [totte] - handle
取る [toru] - take
取る(何かを) [toru(nanika wo)] - get (something)

取る(時間を)、持続する [toru(jikan wo), ijisuru] - take (time), last
手に入れる、とどく、取り出すために [teniireru, todoku, toridasutameni] - get, reach, take something out
手配する、予約する [tehaisuru, yoyakusuru] - arrange, make an appointment
授業、クラス [jugyou, kurasu] - classes
収まる [osamaru] - settle
修復、修理 [shuufuku, shuuri] - renovation, repairs
拾う、ピックアップする、持ち去る [hirou, pikkuappusuru, mochisaru] - pick up, take away
終わらせる [owaraseru] - do (finish)
集める、収集する [atsumeru, shuushuusuru] - collect / gather together, gather
住む [sumu] - live
柔らかい [yawarakai] - soft
渋滞 [juutai] - traffic jam
宿泊施設、アパート [shukuhakushisetsu, apa-to] - accommodation, apartment
出て行く [deteiku] - go out, get out
出口 [deguchi] - exit
準備する [junbisuru] - prepare oneself
暑い [atsui] - hot
書きとめる [kakitomeru] - write down
書く [kaku] - write (down)
書く(チェックを) [kaku(chekku wo)] - write out (a check)
助ける、手伝う [tasukeru, tetsudau] - help
女の子、（女性） [onnanoko, josei] - girl
女性 [josei] - woman
小さい [chiisai] - small
小さいピース [chiisaipi-su] - a little piece

小さいラグ、マット [chiisairagu, matto] - little rug, mat
小さなテーブル [chiisanate-buru] - little table
少し、いくつか [sukoshi, ikutsuka] - a few, little, some
少し、少量の [sukoshi, suuryouno] - a bit, a little
床 [yuka] - floor
招待する [shoutaisuru] - invite
消費する(時間を) [rouhisuru(jikan wo)] - spend (time)
笑う [warau] - laugh
上に [ueni] - on top of, over, above
上に行く、昇る、上がる [ueni iku, noboru, agaru] - go up, ascend, rise
乗る、行く [noru, iku] - ride, go
場所 [basho] - place
情報、インフォメーション [jouhou, infome-shon] - information
職業、専門職 [shokugyou, senmonshoku] - profession
色 [iro] - color
食べる [taberu] - eat
食べ物 [tabemono] - food
食器 [shokki] - dishes
食料品店 [shokuryouhinten] - grocery
信号 [shingou] - traffic lights
寝る [neru] - sleep
心地の良い [kokochinoyoi] - comfortable
新しい [atarashii] - new
新しくない [atarashikunai] - not new
新聞 [shinbunshi] - newspaper
真っすぐ [massugu] - straight
真ん中、〜の途中 [mannaka, 〜notochuu] - in the middle
人 [hito] - person
人々 [hitobito] - people
人生 [jinsei] - life

図書館 [toshokan] - library
水 [mizu] - water
数字、番号 [suuji, bangou] - number
数式 [suushiki] - formula
成功する、無事にすむ [Seikousuru, bujinisumu] - succeed, go off well
生 [nama] - raw
生徒 [seito] - student, pupil
生物学 [seibutsugaku] - biology
製品、食品 [seihin, shokuhin] - products, food
請求書、料金 [seikyuusho, ryoukin] - bill
青 [ao] - blue
静か [shizuka] - quiet
静かに [shizukani] - quietly
石鹸 [sekken] - soap
赤 [aka] - red
切り落とす [kiriotosu] - cut off
切る [kiru] - cut
説明する [setsumeisuru] - explain
絶対〜しない [zettai〜shinai] - never
先生、インストラクター [sensei, insutorakuta-] - teacher, instructor
専門家、プロフェッショナル [senmonka, purofesshonaru] - professional
川 [kawa] - river
洗う、洗濯する、きれいにする [arau, sentakusuru, kireinisuru] - wash, launder, clean
洗濯、洗う [sentaku, arau] - washing
洗濯機、〜洗機、洗っている [sentakuki, 〜senki, aratteiru] - washer, washing
洗濯物、下着、リネン [sentakumono, shitagi, rinen] - laundry, underwear, linen
洗面台 [senmendai] - washbasin
船 [fune] - ship

選ぶ [erabu] - choose
全て [subete] - everything
全ての [subeteno] - every
全体、すべて [zentai, subete] - whole
祖父、年を取った男性 [sofu, toshi wo totta dansei] - grandfather, old man
祖母、年を取った女性 [sofu, toshi wo totta josei] - grandmother, old woman
素晴らしい [subarashii] - excellent
窓 [mado] - window
走る [hashiru] - run
測る [hakaru] - weigh
足す、追加する [tasu, tsuikasuru] - add
続く [tsuzuku] - continue
他の [hokano] - other
太陽 [taiyou] - sun
待つ [motsu] - wait
袋 [fukuro] - packet
代理店、紹介所 [dairiten, shoukaijo] - agency
大きい [ookii] - big
大きくない [ookikunai] - not big
大学 [daigaku] - university
大学の生徒、大学生 [daigakuno seito, daigakusei] - university student
大通り [oodoori] - boulevard
沢山、とても [takusan, totemo] - many, a lot
棚、シェルフ [tana, sherufu] - shelf
誰 [dare] - who
誰か [dareka] - someone
誰の [dareno] - whose
探す [sagasu] - search, look for
探偵 [tantei] - detective
断る [kotowaru] - refuse
暖かい [atatakai] - warm
男性 [dansei] - male, man
値段 [nedan] - price

知り合いになる、習得する、習う [shiriaininaru, shuutokusuru, narau] - get acquainted, learn
知る [shiru] - know
地球、地面、土 [chikyuu, jimen, tsuchi] - earth, ground, soil
地図、マップ [chizu, mappu] - map
地理学 [chirigaku] - geography
置く [oku] - put (down)
茶色 [chairo] - brown
着替える [kigaeru] - get dressed
中、中に [naka, nakani] - in / inside, into
中央 [chuuou] - center, central
昼食 [chuushoku] - lunch
昼食を食べる [choushoku wo taberu] - have lunch
注ぎ入れる [sosogiireru] - pour in
注ぐ [sosogu] - pour
注意深く、丁寧に [chuuibukaku, teineini] - carefully, attentively
注文する [chuumonsuru] - order
喋る [shaberu] - speak
朝 [asa] - morning
朝食 [choushoku] - breakfast
朝食を食べる [choushoku wo taberu] - have breakfast
町 [machi] - city
町の広場 [machinohiroba] - city square
長い、長い間 [nagai, nagaiaida] - long, for a long time
鳥 [tori] - bird
通す/まで [toosu/made] - through / in (time)
通路、セクション [tsuuro, sekushon] - aisle (in a store), section
定規 [jougi] - ruler
庭 [niwa] - garden
提案 [teian] - suggestion
提案する、提供する [teiansuru, teikyousuru] - suggest, offer

提出する、戻す [teishutsusuru, modosu] - give in, return
適切な、適した [tekisetsuna, tekishita] - suitable, fitting
天井 [tenjou] - ceiling
天気 [tenki] - weather
店 [mise] - store, shop
電子レンジ [denshirenji] - microwave
電話 [denwa] - phone, telephone
電話する [denwasuru] - call, phone
土曜日 [doyoubi] - Saturday
盗む [nusumu] - steal
答え [kotae] - answer
到着する [touchakusuru] - arrive, get to
踏みつける [fumitsukeru] - trample
頭 [atama] - head
働く、仕事 [hataraku, shigoto] - work
働く人 [hatarakuhito] - worker
動く、引っ越す [ugoku, hikkosu] - move
動く、機能する [ugoku, kinousuru] - work, function
動物 [doubutsu] - animal
同行する [doukousuru] - accompany
道、行き方 [michi, ikikata] - path, way
道、道路 [michi, douro] - street, road
読む [yomu] - read
届く [todoku] - reach
肉 [niku] - meat
肉体労働 [nikutairoudou] - physical work
日 [hi] - day
日曜日 [nichiyoubi] - Sunday
乳、牛乳 [nyuu, gyuunyuu] - dairy, milk
入る [hairu] - enter
入口 [iriguchi] - entry, entrance
熱い [atsui] - hot
年 [toshi] - year
年上 [toshiue] - older
年齢 [nenrei] - age

燃やす [moyasu] - burn
能力、スキル [nouryoku, sukiru] - skill
買う [kau] - buy
売られる [urareru] - be sold
売る [uru] - sell
白 [shiro] - white
箱 [hako] - box
半分 [hanbun] - half
彼/彼女/それ [kare/kanojo/sore] - he/she/it
彼に、彼を、彼の [kareni, karewo, kareno] - him, his
彼ら(複数) [karera (fukusuu)] - they
疲れる [tsukareru] - get tired
飛ぶ [tobu] - fly
飛行機 [hikouki] - airplane
飛行場 [hikoujou] - airport
美術館 [bijutsukan] - museum
必要 [hitsuyou] - necessary
必要がある、しなければならない [hitsuyouga aru, shinakerebanaranai] - be necessary, need to
病気である [byoukidearu] - be sick
病気になる [byoukininaru] - get sick
苗字 [myouji] - last name
不動産 [fudousan] - real estate
怖い [kowai] - scary
普段、いつも [fudan, itsumo] - normally, usually
部屋 [heya] - room
払う [harau] - pay
物 [mono] - thing
物理学 [butsurigaku] - physics
分 [fun] - minute
噴水 [funsui] - fountain
聞く、尋ねる [kiku, tazuneru] - ask
平和;世界 [heiwa, sekai] - peace; world
壁 [kabe] - wall
勉強する、学ぶ [benkyousuru, manabu] - study, learn

弁護士 [bengoshi] - lawyer
保険 [hoken] - insurance
歩いて [aruite] - on foot
歩く、行く [aruku, iku] - walk, go
歩道 [hodou] - sidewalk
方向 [houkou] - direction
忙しい [isogashii] - busy
冒険 [bouken] - adventure
本 [hon] - book
無言で、静かに [mugonde, shizukani] - without speaking, silently
名前 [namae] - name
名前で呼ぶ、名前をつける [namaede yobu, namae wo tsukeru] - call, name
明かり、電気 [akari, denki] - light
明るい [akarui] - bright
明日 [ashita] - tomorrow
面白い、興味深い [omoshiroi, kyoumibukai] - interesting, funny
木 [ki] - tree
木々、草木 [kigi, kusaki] - greenery
木製の [mokuseino] - wooden
戻る、背中 [modoru, senaka] - back, return
夜 [yoru] - evening
夜に [yoruni] - in the evening
野菜 [yasai] - vegetable
約束 [yakusoku] - promise
友達 [tomodachi] - friend
遊ぶ [asobu] - play
郵便局 [yuubinkyoku] - post office

洋服、ローブ [youfuku, ro-bu] - clothing, robe
用意する、用意された [youisuru, youisareta] - ready, prepared
用意する、料理する [youisuru, ryourisuru] - prepare, cook
欲しい [hoshii] - want
浴びる(シャワーを)、(薬を)飲む [abiru(shawa- wo), (kusuri wo) nomu] - take (a shower, medicine etc.)
落ち着いて [ochitsuite] - calm(ly)
卵 [tamago] - egg
立つ [tatsu] - stand
立てる(垂直に) [tateru(suichokuni)] - put (vertically)
旅行 [ryokou] - travel
両親 [ryoushin] - parents
良い、上手い [yoi, umai] - good, well
良くなる [yokunaru] - better
緑 [midori] - green
冷たい、寒い [tsumetai, samui] - cold
冷蔵庫 [reizouko] - refrigerator
歴史 [rekishi] - history
列 [retsu] - line, queue
列車 [ressha] - train
廊下、通路 [rouka, tsuuro] - hall
話し合う、議論する [hanashiau, gironsuru] - discuss
話す、喋る [hanasu, shaberu] - talk, tell, chat
腕時計 [udedokei] - watch

英日辞書
English-Japanese dictionary

able to, can - できる、することができる [dekiru, surukotoga dekiru]
about - やく [yaku]
accommodation, apartment - 宿泊施設、アパート [shukuhakushisetsu, apa-to]
accompany - 同行する [doukousuru]
across from - 〜の向かいに [〜no mukaini]
act, work - 行動する、〜する [koudousuru, 〜suru]
active - アクティブ [akutibu]
add - 足す、追加する [tasu, tsuikasuru]
address - アドレス、住所 [adoresu, juusho]
adventure - 冒険 [bouken]
after - 〜の後 [〜no ato]
afterwards, then - その後、そして [sonoato, soshite]
age - 年齢 [nenrei]
agency - 代理店、紹介所 [dairiten, shoukaijo]
agent - エージェント [e-jento]
agree - 賛成する [sanseisuru]
airplane - 飛行機 [hikouki]
airport - 飛行場 [hikoujou]
aisle (in a store), section - 通路、セクション [tsuuro, sekushon]
alcoholic - アルコールの [aruko-runo]
all - すべて [subete]
along - 〜に沿って [〜ni sotte]
already - すでに [sudeni]
also, too - 〜も [〜mo]
always - いつも [itsumo]
among - の間に [no aidani]
and - そして [soshite]
animal - 動物 [doubutsu]

announcement, ad - アナウンス [anaunsu]
answer - 答え [kotae]
any, some - いくつか、いくらか [ikutsuka, ikuraka]
apartment, flat - アパート [apa-to]
apple - りんご [ringo]
approach - 近づく [chikazuku]
area, site - エリア、地域 [eria, chiiki]
armchair - アームチェア [a-muchea]
around - 〜ごろ [〜goro]
arrange, make an appointment - 手配する、予約する [tehaisuru, yoyakusuru]
arrive, get to - 到着する [touchakusuru]
ask - 聞く、尋ねる [kiku, tazuneru]
at, near - 〜で、〜の近くで、〜のそばで [〜de, 〜no chikakude, 〜no sobade]
at home - 家で [iede]
auditorium, class-room - 講義室、教室 [kougishitsu, kyoushitsu]
automobile, car - 自動車、車 [jidousha, kuruma]
back - 戻る、背中 [modoru, senaka]
baggage - 荷物 [nimotsu]
baloney, kielbasa, sausage - ばかげたこと、キィエルバサ、ソーセージ [bakagetakoto, kiierubasa, so-se-ji]
banana - バナナ [banana]
bank - 銀行 [ginkou]
bar - バー [ba-]
basket - バスケット [basuketto]
basketball - バスケットボール [basukettobo-ru]
bathroom - トイレ [toire] / バスルーム [basuru-mu]
bathtub - バスタブ [basutabu]
be - 〜である [〜de aru]

be (located) - 〜に位置する, 〜にある [〜ni ichisuru, 〜niaru]
beach - ビーチ、砂浜、(川辺の)浜 [bi-chi, (kawabeno)hama]
because - なぜなら [nazenara]
become - 〜になる [〜ninaru]
bed - ベッド [beddo]
before, earlier - 〜の前、より早く [〜no mae, yorihayaku]
beginning - 始まり [hajimari]
behind, for - 〜の後ろ、〜のため [〜no ushiro, 〜no tame]
beige - ベージュ [be-ju]
bell, ring - ベル、リング [beru, ringu]
better - 良くなる [yokunaru]
between - の間 [no aida]
big - 大きい [ookii]
bill - 請求書、料金 [seikyuusho, ryoukin]
biology - 生物学 [seibutsugaku]
bird - 鳥 [tori]
bit, a little - 少し、少量の [sukoshi, suuryouno]
black - 黒 [kuro]
blender - ブレンダー [burenda-]
blue - 青 [ao]
board - 黒板 [kokuban]
boil, brew - ふっとうする、ゆでる、いれる [futtousuru, yuderu, ireru]
book - 本 [hon]
born - 産まれる [umareru]
bottle - ボトル [botoru]
boulevard - 大通り [oodoori]
box - 箱 [hako]
bread - パン [pan]
bread roll, bun - ロールパン、コッペパン、バン [ro-rupan, koppepan, ban]
break - 壊す [kowasu]
breakfast - 朝食 [choushoku]
bridge - 橋 [hashi]

bright - 明るい [akarui]
bring, carry - 持ってくる、運ぶ [mottekuru, hakobu]
brother - 兄弟 [kyoudai]
brown - 茶色 [chairo]
brush - ブラシ [burashi]
Brussels - ブリュッセル [buryusseru]
burn - 燃やす [moyasu]
bus - バス [basu]
busy - 忙しい [isogashii]
but, while, and - しかし・けれども、〜の間、そして [shikashi, keredomo, 〜no aida, soshite]
buy - 買う [kau]
cabbage - キャベツ [kyabetsu]
cafe - カフェ [kafe]
cake, dessert - ケーキ、デザート [ke-ki, deza-to]
call - 電話する [denwasuru]
call (by phone) - (電話を)かける [(denwa wo)kakeru]
call, name - 名前で呼ぶ、名前をつける [namaede yobu, namae wo tsukeru]
calm(ly) - 落ち着いて [ochitsuite]
car service - 車のサービス [kurumano sa-bisu]
careful - 気を付ける、注意する [ki wo tsukeru, chuuisuru]
carefully, attentively - 注意深く、丁寧に [chuuibukaku, teineini]
carpet - カーペット [ka-petto]
carrot - ニンジン [ninjin]
carry - 運ぶ、抱える [hakobu, kakaeru]
cash - 現金 [genkin]
cashier, teller - 会計係 [kaikeigakari]
cat - ねこ [neko]
ceiling - 天井 [tenjou]
center, central - 中央 [chuuou]
chair - 椅子 [isu]
chalk - チョーク [cho-ku]

chandelier - シャンデリア [shanderia]
checkout, cash register - 会計、レジ [kaikei, reji]
cheese - チーズ [chi-zu]
chicken - にわとり、チキン [niwatori, chikin]
chickens - チキン [chikin]
child - 子供 [kodomo]
choose - 選ぶ [erabu]
cinema, movie theater - 映画館 [eigakan]
city - 町 [machi]
city square - 町の広場 [machinohiroba]
classes - 授業、クラス [jugyou, kurasu]
clean, tidy up - きれい、きれいにする、かたづける [kirei, kireinisuru, katazukeru]
clinic - クリニック [kurinikku]
clothing, robe - 洋服、ローブ [youfuku, ro-bu]
club - クラブ [kurabu]
coffee - コーヒー [ko-hi-]
coffee table - コーヒーテーブル [ko-hi-te-buru]
coffeemaker - コーヒーメーカー [ko-hi-me-ka-]
cold - 冷たい、寒い [tsumetai, samui]
collect / gather together, gather - 集める、収集する [atsumeru, shuushuusuru]
collection - コレクション [korekushon]
color - 色 [iro]
comedy - コメディー [komedi-]
comfortable - 心地の良い [kokochinoyoi]
commercial, advertisement - コマーシャル、広告 [koma-sharu, koukoku]
computer - コンピューター [konpyu-ta-]
consultant - コンサルタント [konsarutanto]

continue - 続く [tsuzuku]
cookie - クッキー [kukki-]
corner - 角 [kado]
cost - 〜がかかる、値段 [〜ga kakaru, nedan]
country - 国 [kuni]
cozy, comfortable - ぬくもりのある、心地の良い [nukumorinoaru, kokochinoyoi]
cry - 泣く [naku]
cucumber - きゅうり [kyuuri]
cup - コップ [koppu]
cupboard, wardrobe, bookcase - カップボード、たんす、本棚 [kappubo-do, tansu]
cut - 切る [kiru]
cut off - 切り落とす [kiriotosu]
dad - パパ [papa]
dairy, milk - 乳、牛乳 [nyuu, gyuunyuu]
dark - 暗い [kurai]
data, information - データ、情報 [de-ta, jouhou]
day - 日 [hi]
dean's office - 学長室 [gakuchoushitsu]
decide - 決定する [ketteisuru]
decision - 決定、決断 [kettei, ketsudan]
dentist - 歯医者 [haisha]
design - デザイン [dezain]
detective - 探偵 [tantei]
different, various - 違う、様々な [chigau, samazamana]
dining room - ダイニングルーム [daininguru-mu]
direction - 方向 [houkou]
dirty - 汚い [kitanai]
discuss - 話し合う、議論する [hanashiau, gironsuru]
dish - 皿 [sara]
dishes - 食器 [shokki]

display, set out - ディスプレイ、陳列する [disupurei, chinretsusuru]
do (finish) - 終わらせる [owaraseru]
do, carry out - する、運び出す [suru, hakobidasu]
doctor, physician - 医者、医師 [isha, ishi]
dog - 犬 [inu]
door - ドア [doa]
drawer, box - たんす、箱 [tansu, hako]
drink - 飲む [nomu]
drive, transport - 運転する、運送する [untensuru, unsousuru]
drive out - 運転して出て行く [untenshite deteiku]
driver - ドライバー、運転手 [doraiba-, untenshu]
driving license - 運転免許 [untenmenkyo]
drugstore - ドラッグストア [doraggusutoa]
dryer - ドライヤー [doraiya-]
Dutch - オランダの [orandano]
Dutchman - オランダ人 [orandajinno]
earn - 稼ぐ [kasegu]
earth, ground, soil - 地球、地面、土 [chikyuu, jimen, tsuchi]
eat - 食べる [taberu]
education - 教育 [kyouiku]
egg - 卵 [tamago]
eight - 8、八 [hachi, hachi]
eight hundred - 800、八百 [happyaku, happyakua]
eighteen - 18、十八 [juuhachi, juuhachi]
elevator - エレベーター [erebe-ta-]
employment, job - 雇用、仕事、職 [koyou, shigoto, shoku]
empty - 空 [kara]
England - イギリス [igirisu]
English - 英語 [eigo]

Englishwoman - イギリスの女性 [igirisuno josei]
enough - 間に合う、〜が十分 [maniau, 〜ga juubun]
enter - 入る [hairu]
enter into a contract - 契約する [keiyakusuru]
entry, entrance - 入口 [iriguchi]
Euro - ユーロ [yu-ro]
evening - 夜 [yoru]
every - 全ての [subeteno]
everything - 全て [subete]
excellent - 素晴らしい [subarashii]
exit - 出口 [deguchi]
expensive - 高い [takai]
experience - 経験 [keiken]
explain - 説明する [setsumeisuru]
family - 家族 [kazoku]
far (away), at a long distance - 遠く、長い距離の [tooku, nagaikyorino]
father - お父さん [otousan]
faucet, tap - 蛇口、栓 [jaguchi, sen]
feel - 感じる、調子 [kanjiru, choushi]
few, some - 少し、いくつか [sukoshi, ikutsuka]
fifteen - 15、十五 [juugo, juugo]
fill out - 記入する [kinyuusuru]
filled out - 記入した [kinyuushita]
film - フィルム [firumu]
find - 見つける [mitsukeru]
fireplace - だんろ [danro]
first - 始めに、1番 [hajimeni, ichiban]
fish - 魚 [sakana]
five - 5、五 [go, go]
flakes, cereal - シリアル [shiriaru]
flight - フライト、飛行 [furaito, hikou]
floor, storey - 床、階 [yuka, kai]
flower - 花 [hana]
fly - 飛ぶ [tobu]

following, next - 次の、次 [tsugino, tsugi]
food - 食べ物 [tabemono]
for - 〜のため、〜にとって [〜notame, 〜nitotte]
fork - フォーク [fo-ku]
formula - 、数式 [suushiki]
forty - 40、四十 [yonjuu, yonjuu]
fountain - 噴水 [funsui]
four - 4、四 [yon, yon]
fourth - 4番 [yonban]
Frank - フランク [furanku]
free - 自由、タダ [jiyuu, tada]
free(ly), fluently - 自由に、ペラペラに [jiyuuni, peraperani]
French - フランス語 [furansugo]
Friday - 金曜日 [kinyoubi]
friend - 友達 [tomodachi]
from, out of - 〜から、〜の外へ [〜kara, 〜no sotohe]
from the beginning - 始めから [hajimekara]
from where - 〜から、どこから [〜kara, dokokara]
fruit - 果物 [kajitsu]
full - いっぱい [ippai]
function - 動く、機能する [ugoku, kinousuru]
funny - 面白い [omoshiroi]
furniture - 家具 [kagu]
further - さらに遠く [saranitooku]
game - ゲーム [ge-mu]
garage - ガレージ、車庫 [gare-ji, shako]
garden - 庭 [niwa]
gas - ガス [gasu]
geography - 地理学 [chirigaku]
German - ドイツの [doitsuno]
get (something) - (何かを)取る [(nanika wo) toru]
get, reach, take something out - 手に入れる、とどく、取り出すために [teniireru, todoku, toridasutameni]
get a job - 仕事につく [shigotoni tsuku]
get acquainted, learn - 知り合いになる、習得する、習う [shiriaininaru, shuutokusuru, narau]
get dressed - 着替える [kigaeru]
get sick - 病気になる [byoukininaru]
get tired - 疲れる [tsukareru]
get treated - 治療してもらう [chiryoushitemorau]
get up - 起きる、起き上がる [okiru, okiagaru]
girl - 女の子、（女性）[onnanoko, josei]
give - あげる、渡す [ageru, watasu]
give in, return - 提出する、戻す [teishutsusuru, modosu]
glass - ガラス [garasu]
glasses - 眼鏡 [megane]
go, walk - 行く、散歩をする、歩く [iku, sanpo wo suru, aruku]
go into - 〜に入る [〜ni hairu]
go out, get out - 出て行く [dęteiku]
go up, ascend, rise - 上に行く、昇る、上がる [ueni iku, noboru, agaru]
go/ride away - 行く/乗って行く [iku/notteiku]
good - 良い [yoi]
grab - つかむ [tsukamu]
grandfather, old man - 祖父、年を取った男性 [sofu, toshi wo totta dansei]
grandmother, old woman - 祖母、年を取った女性 [sofu, toshi wo totta josei]
grape(s) - ぶどう [budou]
gray - グレー [gure-]
Great Britain - 英国 [eikoku]
green - 緑 [midori]
greenery - 木々、草木 [kigi, kusaki]

grocery - 食料品店 [shokuryouhinten]
grow - 育つ、大きくなる [sodatsu, ookikunaru]
guest - ゲスト [gesuto]
half - 半分 [hanbun]
hall - 廊下、通路 [rouka, tsuuro]
hamburger - ハンバーガー [hanba-ga-]
handle - ハンドル、取っ手 [handoru, totte]
hang - かける、かかる、つるさがる [kakeru, kakaru, tsurusagaru]
have, own - 持つ、所有する、飼う [motsu, shoyuusuru, kau]
have breakfast - 朝食を食べる [choushoku wo taberu]
have lunch - 昼食を食べる [choushoku wo taberu]
have to, be obliged - しなければならない、せざるをえない [shinakerebanaranai, sezaruwoenai]
he/she/it - 彼/彼女/それ [kare/kanojo/sore]
head - 頭 [atama]
hello - こんにちは [konnichiha]
help - 助ける、手伝う [tasukeru, tetsudau]
here (direction) - ここ(方向) [koko (houkou)]
hi, hello - こんにちは [konnichiwa]
high - 高い [takai]
highway - 高速道路、ハイウェイ [kousokudouro, haiwei]
hill, mountain - 丘、山 [oka, yama]
him, his - 彼に、彼を、彼の [kareni, karewo, kareno]
history - 歴史 [rekishi]
homeward - 家へ帰る道 [ie he kaerumichi]
honey - ハチミツ [hachimitsu]
hot - 暑い [atsui]
hotel - ホテル [hoteru]
hour - 時間 [jikan]
house/home - 家、家庭 [ie, katei]
how - どうやって [douyatte]
how many years - 何年 [nannen]
how much - どれくらい、いくら [dorekurai, ikura]
I - 私 [watashi]
ice cream - アイスクリーム [aisukuri-mu]
in - 〜にある、〜の中 [〜ni aru, 〜no naka]
in, into - 中、中に [naka, nakani]
in order to, so that - 〜するため [〜surutame]
in the evening - 夜に [yoruni]
in the middle - 真ん中、〜の途中 [mannaka, 〜notochuu]
indicate - 指し示す [sashishimesu]
indicated - 指し示された [sashishimesareta]
inexpensive - 安い [yasui]
information - 情報、インフォメーション [jouhou, infome-shon]
inside - 中 [naka]
insurance - 保険 [hoken]
interesting - 面白い、興味深い [omoshiroi, kyoumibukai]
invite - 招待する [shoutaisuru]
Italian (person) - イタリア人 [itariajin]
Italy - イタリア [itaria]
juice - ジュース [ju-su]
key - キー、鍵 [ki-, kagi]
kiosk - キオスク [kiosuku]
kitchen - キッチン [kicchin]
knife - ナイフ [naifu]
knock - ノック [nokku]
know - 知る [shiru]
lake - 湖 [mizuumi]
lamp - ランプ [ranpu]

language / tongue - 言語/言葉 [gengo/kotoba]
laptop - ラップトップ [rapputoppu]
last name - 苗字 [myouji]
laugh - 笑う [warau]
laundromat, launderette - コインランドリー [koinrandori-]
laundry, underwear, linen - 洗濯物、下着、リネン [sentakumono, shitagi, rinen]
lawyer - 弁護士 [bengoshi]
lead, drive - 案内する、運転する [annaisuru, untensuru]
leather - 革 [kawa]
left, stay - 残される、残る [nokosareru, nokoru]
lemon - レモン [remon]
librarian - 司書 [shisho]
library - 図書館 [toshokan]
lie - 横になっている [yokoninatteiru]
life - 人生 [jinsei]
light - 明かり、電気、光 [akari, denki, hikari]
like, appeal - 好き、好む [suki, konomu]
like this, so - このように、なので [konoyouni, nanode]
line, queue - 列 [retsu]
listen to - 〜を聞く [〜wo kiku]
liter - リットル [rittoru]
little, few - 少し、いくつか [sukoshi, ikutsuka]
little piece - 小さいピース [chiisaipi-su]
little rug, mat - 小さいラグ、マット [chiisairagu, matto]
little table - 小さなテーブル [chiisanate-buru]
live - 住む [sumu]
living room - リビングルーム [ribinguru-mu]
loader, stevedore - 荷物を積み込む人、港湾労働者 [nimotsu wo tsumikomuhito, kouwanroudousha]
long, for a long time - 長い、長い間 [nagai, nagaiaida]
look like - (に)似ている [(ni) niteiru]
love - 愛、愛する、好き [ai, aisuru, suki]
lunch - 昼食 [chuushoku]
machine - 機械 [kikai]
magazine - 雑誌 [zasshi]
make - 作る [tsukuru]
male - 男性 [dansei]
man - 男性 [dansei]
manager, head - 経営者、社長 [keieisha, shachou]
many, a lot - 沢山、とても [takusan, totemo]
map - 地図、マップ [chizu, mappu]
married - 結婚している [kekkonshiteiru]
maybe - かもしれない [kamoshirenai]
meat - 肉 [niku]
mechanic - メカニック [mekanikku]
meet - 会う [au]
memorial, monument - 記念碑 [kinenhi]
metal - 金属 [kinzoku]
metro, subway - メトロ、地下鉄 [metoro, chikatetsu]
microwave - 電子レンジ [denshirenji]
milk - 牛乳 [gyuunyuu]
minibus - ミニバス [minibasu]
minute - 分 [fun]
mirror - 鏡 [kagami]
mixer - ミキサー [mikisa-]
Mom - ママ [mama]
money - お金 [okane]
month - 月 [tsuki]
more, still - もっと、よりおおくの、まだ [motto, yoriookuno, mada]

morning - 朝 [asa]
motorcycle, motorbike - バイク、オートバイ [baiku, o-tobai]
move - 動く、引っ越す [ugoku, hikkosu]
move (to change address) - 引っ越す(住所を変える) [hikkosu (juusho wo kaeru)]
museum - 美術館 [bijutsukan]
mushroom - マッシュルーム、きのこ [masshuru-mu, kinoko]
my (mine) - 私の(私の物) [watashino (watashinomono)]
name - 名前 [namae]
napkin - ナプキン [napukin]
Naples - ナポリ [napori]
national - 国民 [kokumin]
nationality - 国籍 [kokuseki]
near - 〜の近く、〜のそば [〜no chikaku, no soba]
necessary - 必要 [hitsuyou]
need to - 必要がある、しなければならない [hitsuyouga aru, shinakerebanaranai]
neighbor - 近所 [kinjo]
never - 絶対〜しない [zettai〜shinai]
new - 新しい [atarashii]
newspaper - 新聞 [shinbunshi]
next to, near - の隣に、近く [no tonarini, chikaku]
nine - 9、九 [kyuu, kyuu]
nineteen - 19、十九 [juukyuu, juukyuu]
no; there isn't, there aren't - いいえ;〜は(が)ない [iie, 〜ha(ga) nai]
noisily - うるさく [urusaku]
noisy - うるさい [urusai]
normally, usually - 普段、いつも [fudan, itsumo]
not - 〜でない [〜denai]
not big - 大きくない [ookikunai]

not far - そう遠くない [soutookunai]
not long ago, recently - そう遠くない昔、最近 [soutookunaimukashi, saikin]
not new - 新しくない [atarashikunai]
not tall - 高くない [takakunai]
notebook, copybook - ノートブック [notobukku]
now - 今 [ima]
number - 数字、番号 [suuji, bangou]
nursery - 育児室 [takujishitsu]
occupy - を占める [wo shimeru]
ocean - 海 [umi]
of course - もちろん [mochiron]
office - オフィス、事務所 [ofisu, jimusho]
often - よく [yoku]
old - 古い [furui]
older - 年上 [toshiue]
on - 〜の上 [〜no ue]
on foot - 歩いて [aruite]
on the left - 左に [hidarini]
on the right - 右に [migini]
on top of, over, above - 上に [ueni]
one - 1、一 [ichi, ichi]
one and a half - 1個半 [ikkohan]
only, just - 〜だけ、ただ [〜dake, tada]
open - 開く、開ける [hiraku, akeru]
or - または [mataha]
orange - オレンジ [orenji]
order - 注文する [chuumonsuru]
other - 他の [hokano]
our(s) - 私たちの [watashitachino]
outside - 外 [soto]
over, along - の上、に沿って [no ue, ni sotte]
owner - オーナー [o-na-]
package - パッケージ [pakke-ji]
packet - 袋 [fukuro]
page - ページ [pe-ji]

pair - ペア [pea]
paper - 紙 [kami]
parents - 両親 [ryoushin]
park - 公園 [kouen]
part-time - パートタイム、非常勤 [pa-totaimu, hijoukin]
part-time job - パートタイムの仕事、アルバイト [pa-totaimuno shigoto, arubaito]
pass - パス [pasu]
passage; fare - 通路、運賃 [tsuuro, unchin]
passport - パスポート [pasupo-to]
past, near - を通り過ぎる、近く [wo toorisugiru, chikaku]
pasta, macaroni - パスタ、マカロニ [pasuta, makaroni]
path, way - 道、行き方 [michi, ikikata]
pay - 払う [harau]
peace; world - 平和;世界 [heiwa, sekai]
peach - もも [momo]
pencil - 鉛筆 [enpitsu]
people - 人々 [hitobito]
period - 期間 [kikan]
person - 人 [hito]
personal - 個人の [kojinno]
phone - 電話、電話する [denwa, denwasuru]
photograph - 写真 [shashin]
physical work - 肉体労働 [nikutairoudou]
physics - 物理学 [butsurigaku]
pick up, take away - 拾う、ピックアップする、持ち去る [hirou, pikkuappusuru, mochisaru]
picture - 写真、絵 [shashin, e]
piece - 一片 [ippen]
pillow - まくら [makura]
pineapple - パイナップル [painappuru]
pizza - ピザ [piza]

place - 場所 [basho]
placement, employment - 仕事紹介、雇用 [shigotoshoukai, koyou]
plastic - プラスチック [purasuchikku]
plate - 皿、プレート [sara, pure-to]
play - 遊ぶ [asobu]
police - 警察 [keisatsu]
policeman - 警察官 [keisatsukan]
polyethylene, plastic - ポリエチレン、プラスチック [poriechiren, purasuchikku]
possible - 可能な、できる [kanouna, dekiru]
post office - 郵便局 [yuubinkyoku]
potato chips - ポテトチップス [potetochippusu]
pour (something fluid) / pour (something loose) - 注ぐ [sosogu]
pour in - 注ぎ入れる [sosogiireru]
prepare, cook - 用意する、料理する [youisuru, ryourisuru]
prepare oneself - 準備する [junbisuru]
pretty, beautiful - かわいい、美しい [kawaii, utsukushii]
price - 値段 [nedan]
probably - おそらく [osoraku]
products, food - 製品、食品 [seihin, shokuhin]
profession - 職業、専門職 [shokugyou, senmonshoku]
professional - 専門家、プロフェッショナル [senmonka, purofesshonaru]
promise - 約束 [yakusoku]
purple - 紫 [murasaki]
purse, bag - ハンドバック、バック [handobakku, bakku]
put (down) - 置く [oku]
put (vertically) - (垂直に)立てる [(suichokuni)tateru]
put on - を乗せる [wo noseru]

questionnaire - 質問事項、質問事項表 [shitsumonjikou, shitsumonjikousho]
quickly - 急いで [isoide]
quiet - 静か [shizuka]
quietly - 静かに [shizukani]
rack, stand - ラック、スタンド [rakku, sutando]
radio - ラジオ [rajio]
rain - 雨 [ame]
raw - 生 [nama]
reach - 届く [todoku]
read - 読む [yomu]
ready, prepared - 用意する、用意された [youisuru, youisareta]
real estate - 不動産 [fudousan]
receipt - レシート [reshi-to]
red - 赤 [aka]
refrigerator - 冷蔵庫 [reizouko]
refuse - 拒否する、断る [kyohisuru, kotowaru]
renovation, repairs - 修復、修理 [shuufuku, shuuri]
rest, relax - 休む、リラックス [yasumu, rirakkusu]
restaurant - レストラン [resutoran]
return - 戻る [modoru]
rice - お米 [okome]
ride, go - 乗る、行く [noru, iku]
right away - すぐに [suguni]
rights - 権利 [kenri]
river - 川 [kawa]
road - 道路 [douro]
roof - 屋根 [yane]
room - 部屋 [heya]
rose - バラ [bara]
roughly, approximately - おおよそ [ooyoso]
round - 丸い [marui]
rubber - ゴム [gomu]
rule - ルール [ru-ru]

ruler - 定規 [jougi]
run - 走る [hashiru]
salmon - サーモン [sa-mon]
sandwich - サンドイッチ [sandoicchi]
Sarah - サラ [sara]
Saturday - 土曜日 [doyoubi]
saucepan - ソースパン [so-supan]
sausage - ソーセージ [so-se-ji]
say goodbye - さよならを言う [sayonara wo iu]
scales - はかり [hakari]
scan - スキャン [sukyan]
scary - 怖い [kowai]
school - 学校 [gakkou]
sea - 海 [umi]
search, look for - 探す [sagasu]
second - 2番 [niban]
see - 見る [miru]
sell - 売る [uru]
settle - 収まる [osamaru]
seven - 7、七 [nana, nana]
Shakespeare - シェイクスピア [sheikusupia]
shelf - 棚、シェルフ [tana, sherufu]
shine - 輝く [kagayaku]
ship - 船 [fune]
shore - 岸 [kishi]
show - 見せる [miseru]
shower - シャワー [shawa-]
sick - 病気である [byoukidearu]
sidewalk - 歩道 [hodou]
single, with space for one person - 一人の、一人用のスペース [hitorino, hitoriyouno supe-su]
sink - シンク [sinku]
sister - 姉妹 [shimai]
sit, sit down - 座る [suwaru]
six - 6、六 [roku, roku]
skill - 能力、スキル [nouryoku, sukiru]

sleep - 寝る [neru]
small - 小さい [chiisai]
so, because of this - 〜なので、だから、それによって [〜nanode, dakara, soreniyotte]
soap - 石鹸 [sekken]
soccer - サッカー [sakka-]
soccer player - サッカー選手 [sakka-senshu]
sociable - 社交的な [shakoutekina]
sofa, couch - ソファー、カウチ [sofa-, kauchi]
soft - 柔らかい [yawarakai]
sold - 売られる [urareru]
someone - 誰か [dareka]
something - 何か [nanika]
sometime / sometimes, some day - 時々、いつか [tokidoki, itsuka]
soon - まもなく [mamonaku]
soup - スープ [su-pu]
sour cream - サワークリーム [sawa-kuri-mu]
spacious - 広い [hiroi]
Spaniard - スペイン人 [supeinjin]
speak - 喋る [shaberu]
spend (time) - (時間を)消費する [(jikan wo) rouhisuru]
spoon - スプーン [supu-n]
staircase - 階段 [kaidan]
stamp - スタンプ [sutanpu]
stand - スタンド、立つ [sutando, tatsu]
start - スタート、開始 [suta-to, kaishi]
station - 駅 [eki]
status - ステータス [sute-tasu]
steal - 盗む [nusumu]
step - ステップ [suteppu]
stop - 止まる [tomaru]
store, shop - 店 [mise]
stove - ストーブ [suto-bu]
straight - 真っすぐ [massugu]

strawberry - いちご [ichigo]
street - 道、道路 [michi, douro]
student, pupil - 生徒 [seito]
study, learn - 勉強する、学ぶ [benkyousuru, manabu]
subject, thing - 議題、もの、物事 [gidai, mono, monogoto]
suburb - 郊外 [kougai]
succeed, go off well - 成功する、無事にすむ [Seikousuru, bujinisumu]
sugar - 砂糖 [satou]
suggest, offer - 提案する、提供する [teiansuru, teikyousuru]
suggestion - 提案 [teian]
suitable, fitting - 適切な、適した [tekisetsuna, tekishita]
sun - 太陽 [taiyou]
Sunday - 日曜日 [nichiyoubi]
supermarket - スーパー [su-pa-]
sweet - 甘い [amai]
swim - 泳ぐ [oyogu]
switch - スイッチ [suicchi]
synopsis, outline - 一覧、概要 [ichiran, gaiyou]
table - テーブル [te-buru]
tablecloth - テーブルクロス [te-burukurosu]
take - 取る [toru]
take (a shower, medicine etc.) - (シャワーを)浴びる、(薬を)飲む [(shawa- wo) abiru, (kusuri wo) nomu]
take (time), last - (時間を)取る、持続する [(jikan wo)toru, ijisuru]
take a walk - 散歩をする [sanpo wo suru]
take by, drive, transport - つかむ、運転する、輸送する [tsukamu, untensuru, yusousuru]
take photos/pictures - 写真を撮る [shashin wo toru]

talk, chat - 話す、喋る [hanasu, shaberu]
tasty - おいしい [oishii]
taxi - タクシー [takushi-]
tea - 紅茶 [koucha]
teach - 教える [oshieru]
teacher, instructor - 先生、インストラクター [sensei, insutorakuta-]
teapot - ティーポット [ti-potto]
technology - テクノロジー [tekunoroji-]
teeth, tooth - 歯 [ha]
telephone - 電話 [denwa]
tell - 言う、教える、話す [iu, oshieru, hanasu]
ten - 10、十 [juu, juu]
test - テスト [tesuto]
textbook - 教科書、テキスト [kyoukasho, tekisuto]
thanks - 感謝する [kanshasuru]
that - あれ [are]
theater - 劇場 [gekijou]
then, later - そして、後で [soshite, atode]
there (direction) - そちら(の方向) [sochira(no houkou)]
there (place) - そこ [soko]
there is, there are - 〜にある、〜がある [〜ni aru, 〜ga aru]
these (plural) - これら(複数) [korera (fukusuu)]
they - 彼ら(複数) [karera (fukusuu)]
thing - 物 [mono]
think - 考える、思う [kangaeru, omou]
third - 3番 [sanban]
thirteen - 13、十三 [juusan, juusan]
thirty - のどが渇く [nodoga kawaku]
this - これ [kore]
three - 3、三 [san, san]
three hundred - 300、三百 [sanbyaku]

through / in (time) - 通す/まで [toosu/made]
ticket - チケット [chiketto]
time - 時間 [jikan]
time(s) (as in "how many times") - （数）回 [(suu)kai]
to - 〜へ [〜he]
toaster - トースター [to-suta-]
today - 今日 [kyou]
together - 一緒に [isshoni]
toilet, bathroom - トイレ、バスルーム [toire, basuru-mu]
tomato - トマト [tomato]
tomorrow - 明日 [ashita]
tooth - 歯 [ha]
tourist - ツアー客 [tsua-kyaku]
towards - 〜の方へ [〜no houhe]
towel - タオル [taoru]
traffic jam - 渋滞 [juutai]
traffic lights - 信号 [shingou]
train - 列車 [ressha]
trample - 踏みつける [fumitsukeru]
transport - 〜へ運送する [〜he unsousuru]
trash, garbage - ゴミ、生ごみ [gomi, namagomi]
travel - 旅行 [ryokou]
treatment - 治療 [chiryou]
tree - 木 [ki]
trolleybus - トロリーバス [torori-basu]
tulip - チューリップ [chu-rippu]
tunnel - トンネル [tonneru]
turn on - スイッチを入れる [suicchi wo ireru]
Tv-set - テレビセット [terebisetto]
twelfth - 12番目 [juunibanme]
twelve - 12、十二 [juuni, juuni]
twenty - 20、二十 [nijuu, nijuu]
two - 2、二 [ni, ni]
under - 〜の下 [〜no shita]

university - 大学 [daigaku]
university student - 大学の生徒、大学生 [daigakuno seito, daigakusei]
until, to - 〜まで [〜made]
us - 私たち [watashitachi]
vacation - 休暇 [kyuuka]
value, price - 価値、価格、値段 [kachi, kakaku, nedan]
vase - かびん [kabin]
vegetable - 野菜 [yasai]
very - とても [totemo]
wagon, carriage, cart - 荷車、カート [niguruma, ka-to]
wait - 待つ [motsu]
waiter - ウェイター [ueita-]
wake up - 起きる [okiru]
walk, go - 歩く、行く [aruku, iku]
wall - 壁 [kabe]
wallet - 財布 [saifu]
want - 欲しい [hoshii]
warm - 暖かい [atatakai]
warm (up) - 温める [atatameru]
wash, launder, clean - 洗う、洗濯する、きれいにする [arau, sentakusuru, kireinisuru]
wash oneself - 自分の体を洗う [jibunno karada wo arau]
washbasin - 洗面台 [senmendai]
washer, washing - 洗濯機、〜洗機、洗っている [sentakuki, 〜senki, aratteiru]
washing - 洗濯、洗う [sentaku, arau]
watch - 腕時計 [udedokei]
water - 水 [mizu]
we - 私たち [watashitachi]
weather - 天気 [tenki]
week - 一週間 [ichishuukan]
weigh - 測る [hakaru]
well - 良い、上手い [yoi, umai]

what - 何 [nani]
when - いつ [itsu]
where - どこ [doko]
where to - どこへ [dokohe]
whether, if - 〜かどうか、もし [〜kadouka, moshi]
which, what - どれ、何 [dore, nani]
white - 白 [shiro]
who - 誰 [dare]
whole - 全体、すべて [zentai, subete]
whose - 誰の [dareno]
why - なぜ、どうして [naze, doushite]
window - 窓 [mado]
wish, desire - 願い、したがる [negai, shitagaru]
with - 〜と一緒に [〜to isshoni]
without - を除いて [wo nozoite]
without speaking, silently - 無言で、静かに [mugonde, shizukani]
woman - 女性 [josei]
wooden - 木製の [mokuseino]
work - 働く、仕事 [hataraku, shigoto]
work hard - 一生懸命働く [isshoukenmei hataraku]
worker - 働く人 [hatarakuhito]
write - 書く [kaku]
write down - 書きとめる [kakitomeru]
write out (a check) - (チェックを)書く [(chekku wo)kaku]
writer - ライター、作家、記者 [raita-, sakka, kisha]
year - 年 [toshi]
years - 何年も [nannenmo]
yellow - 黄色 [kiiro]
yes - はい [hai]
you, your(s) - あなた、あなたの [anata, anatano]

Recommended books

First Japanese Reader for Beginners
Bilingual for Speakers of English
Beginner and Elementary (A1 A2)

This book starts the series of Japanese Graded Readers. The book consists of Beginner and Elementary courses with parallel Japanese-English texts. The author maintains learners' motivation with funny stories about real life situations such as meeting people, studying, job searches, working etc. The method utilizes the natural human ability to remember words used in texts repeatedly and systematically. The second and the following chapters of the Beginner course have only about thirty new words each. The texts are provided with the phonetic transcriptions Furigana and Romaji. The audio tracks are available inclusive online.

First Japanese Reader for Students
Bilingual for Speakers of English
Beginner Elementary (A1 A2)

Each chapter is filled with words that are organized by topic, then used in a story in Japanese. Questions and answers rephrase information and text is repeated in English to aid comprehension. The quick and easy-to-use format organizes many of life's situations from knowing your way around the house, studying at university, or getting a job. The method utilizes the natural human ability to remember words used in texts repeatedly and systematically. The audio tracks are available inclusive on www.lppbooks.com/Japanese/

Learn Japanese Language Through Dialogue
Bilingual for Speakers of English
Beginner Elementary (A1 A2)

The textbook gives you a lot of examples on how questions in Japanese should be formed. It is easy to see the difference between Japanese and English using parallel translation. Common questions and answers used in everyday situations are explained simply enough even for beginners. The audio tracks are available inclusive on www.lppbooks.com/Japanese/

First Japanese Reader for Business
Bilingual for Speakers of English
Beginner Elementary (A1 A2)

First Japanese Reader for Business is a resource that guides readers with the Japanese vocabulary, phrases, and questions that are relevant to many situations in the workplace. With twenty-five chapters on topics from the office to software and supplementary resources including the Japanese/English and English/Japanese dictionaries, it is the book to help the businessperson take their Japanese language knowledge to the professional level. The audio tracks are available inclusive on www.lppbooks.com/Japanese/

First Japanese Medical Reader for Health Professions and Nursing
Bilingual for Speakers of English
Beginner Elementary (A1 A2)

First Japanese Medical Reader for Health Professions and Nursing will give you the words and phrases necessary for helping patients making appointments, informing them of their diagnosis, and their treatment options. Medical specialties range from ENT to dentistry. Supplementary resources include the Japanese/English and English/Japanese dictionaries. Use this book to take your Japanese knowledge to the health professional's level. The audio tracks are available inclusive on www.lppbooks.com/Japanese/

www.ingramcontent.com/pod-product-compliance
Lightning Source LLC
Chambersburg PA
CBHW081917170426
43200CB00014B/2755